"Weak Thing" in Moni Land

"God hath
chosen the weak things . . ."
(1 Corinthians 1:27b)

"Weak Thing" in Moni Land

The Story of
Bill and Gracie Cutts

William A. Cutts

Christian Publications

CAMP HILL, PENNSYLVANIA

Christian Publications
3825 Hartzdale Drive, Camp Hill, PA 17011

The mark of † *vibrant faith*

ISBN: 0-87509-429-5
LOC Catalog Card Number: 90-80454
© 1990 by Christian Publications
All rights reserved
Printed in the United States of America

94 93 92 91   5 4 3 2

Cover illustration
© 1991, Karl Foster

To Gracie:

the young woman who, on a moonlit, midsummer's evening in 1946, crossed the Hudson with me on the old Tarrytown ferry, and who, with me, subsequently crossed many treacherous rivers of Irian Jaya's rugged interior highlands on swinging, jungle-vine bridges, this book is lovingly dedicated.

THE WORK OF

THE CHRISTIAN AND MISSIONARY ALLIANCE

IN IRIAN JAYA, INDONESIA

SHOWING

TRIBAL NAMES, MISSION POSTS & PLACES OF MINISTRY

SORONG

FAK FAK

DOU

NABIRE
Nabire Theological School

WOLANI

Biandoga River

BUGALAGA

Kemandoga River

MONI Dugindoga Rive

Rou

EKARI

HOMEYO

POGAPA

HITADIPA

Moni B

Wissel Lakes

KEBO
Indonesian Bible School

ENAROTALI

Damal E

KEGATA

MAGODE

MOANIMANI

TIGI
Ekari Bible School

TEMBAGAPURA

DAM

EKARI

TEMIKA

MILES

0   5   10   15   20   25

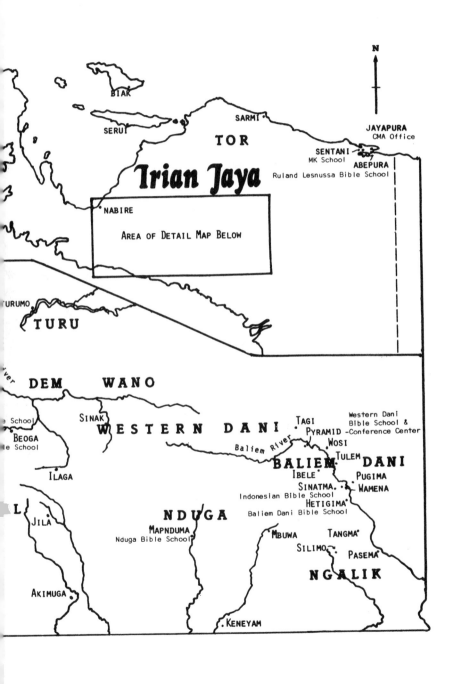

N

BIAK

SERUI

SARMI

JAYAPURA
CMA Office

TOR

SENTANI
MK School

ABEPURA

Irian Jaya

Ruland Lesnussa Bible School

NABIRE

AREA OF DETAIL MAP BELOW

URUMO

TURU

DEM   WANO

River

e School

SINAK

WESTERN DANI

Tagi

Western Dani
Bible School &
-Conference Center

BEOGA
e School

PYRAMID

WOSI

Baliem River

TULEM DANI

ILAGA

BALIEM

IBELE

PUGIMA

SINATMA.

WAMENA

Indonesian Bible School

L

JILA

NDUGA

MAPNDUMA
Nduga Bible School

HETIGIMA

Baliem Dani Bible School

MBUWA

TANGMA

SILIMO

PASEMA

AKIMUGA

NGALIK

KENEYAM

Contents

F o r e w o r d

PSYCHOLOGISTS TEACH, AND PEOPLE generally expect, that anyone who had an unfortunate childhood is destined to run a gauntlet of serious handicaps as an adult. Indeed, some underprivileged children even gear up to exploiting public sympathy for their "handicap." They become practiced failures—professional dependents.

If ever anyone had a ready-made excuse to live out his life as a ward of charity, it was my friend Bill Cutts, author of *"Weak Thing" in Moni Land.* A doctor's decision to sacrifice a baby to save the mother left Bill seriously deformed—but still breathing. Bill could not even walk until he was four years old!

Could such a person rise above pitying himself to minister to others? Could the man who grew from such a child become a pioneer on one of the world's harshest frontiers? Could such a man inspire a barbarous culture to follow Jesus, the Prince of Peace?

In the wisdom of God, Bill Cutts *could!* In the love of God, Bill Cutts *would!* By the grace of God, Bill Cutts *did!*

Reader, prepare yourself! This one-eyed, misshapen servant of Christ with his amazing story may well be the chisel God will use to carve more grace and symmetry into your own spirit!

Don Richardson

Acknowledgments

I am grateful for this opportunity to publicly thank my friends who studied the chapters as they emerged from my word processor and who were kind enough to ask questions and offer suggestions that hopefully ensure worthwhile reading:

Gracie Cutts
Holly Blaubach
Rosalie Lenehan Johnson
David G. Reese
Ted Simonson
Barbara Wulf

Preface

SHORTLY AFTER OUR ARRIVAL from the mission field for the last time in June of 1985, I was assigned to a nine-week missionary deputation tour. I prayed much about the ministry, but it seemed that my Lord didn't give even a hint of what I was to tell the people.

On the platform at the first church of the tour, 10 minutes before I was to stand behind the pulpit, the pastor asked me, "What are you going to talk about?"

I answered honestly, "I don't know."

The pastor introduced me to the congregation. I stood up and at that moment the Lord filled my mouth as I spoke of what He had done in my life. I continued to use the same message throughout the tour. People frequently commented, "Bill, you must write that up."

So here it is. My only purpose for writing this book is to glorify the Lord who loved me and gave Himself for me, whose I am and whom I serve. May the contents of these pages bring great blessing to you.

1

The "Weak Thing"

SWEAT POURED DOWN THE DOCTOR'S FACE as the hands of the clock continued to advance. Close by, the young mother writhed in agony. It was obvious that this would be a very difficult delivery.

Today the solution to such a complication would be simple—a phone call, an ambulance screaming its way to the hospital a few minutes away. But in 1915, hospitals were doorways to death as often as they were doorways to life.

Finally the doctor spoke. "Mr. Cutts, there is no way that both the mother and the baby are going to survive. Whom shall I try to save?"

Five years earlier, a widow had emigrated from England to America with her three children—19-year-old Leonard Cutts and his younger brother and sister. They had settled in Scranton, Pennsylvania. While working for the Scranton Lace Curtain Company, Leonard became acquainted with a fellow worker, Eva Itterly. Courtship ensued, and their marriage followed in 1914.

By August, 1915, Leonard and Eva were living in the village of Chinchilla, a few miles north of Scranton. The young bride and groom had already shared a year of marital bliss and tonight their happiness was to increase with the addition of a new family member.

The doctor's bleak statement was totally unexpected. His devastating question burned into young Leonard's mind. "Whom shall I try to save?"

Len looked down at his beloved wife who tried in vain to suppress her screams as the pressure increased. His mind raced back to the day when she had told him that a little one was on the way. There had been the joy of watching the unborn baby grow. Would it be a boy or a girl? Who would the baby look like? The layette had been lovingly prepared; the tiny garments were all ready. Now the beautiful dream was turning into a horrible nightmare. What kind of a life would it be trying to raise a little one without his cherished Eva?

"Doctor, by all means, try to save my wife."

And so the sentence of death was passed to the baby. The doctor reached for the ugly tools that could place a dead infant on the sheet.

Finally the awful ordeal was over. A baby boy lay there twisted and discolored from bruises, his right eye dangling by its cords on his cheek. But he was breathing! The omnipotent God had plans for that baby.

As the years passed, the tiny, twisted body stretched toward normalcy though never quite attained it. The child's left side developed faster than the right, giving the appearance that half of two different bodies had been fused together. Baby Bill's first faltering steps began not at ten months, nor a year, nor two years, but at four. This representative of *homo erectus* was more often in a heap on the ground.

When God was choosing a missionary to slog through the difficult terrain of interior Irian Jaya, no one would have guessed that He would pick such a misshapen bit of humanity for the job. Or would they? First Corinthians 1:26–29 (KJV) reads: ". . . not many mighty . . . are called: But God hath chosen the . . . weak things of the world to confound the things which are mighty; . . . That no flesh should glory in his presence." Our God is sovereign. He decides to do things no one would expect Him to do and then carries out His plans to perfect completion.

I was the baby just described. Now, in 1989, I am 74 years old. After serving more than 35 years in the interior of Irian Jaya, Indonesia, I look back in amazement at the evidence of my Lord's almighty power throughout the years of my life. He has performed miracle after miracle, enabling me to complete the task to which He called me. I can take no credit for what happened. I can only humbly rejoice at what the sovereign God has been able to do with the "weak thing."

2

The Potter's Wheel

HOW BLESSED ARE THE CHILDREN that grow up in godly homes! Mother had her little family in the nearby church every time the doors were open. My earliest recollections are of being in Sunday school without fail and at church services when the circuit-riding preacher was in town once every two weeks.

After my birth, my parents moved from Chinchilla to Binghamton, New York, where Dad worked in a roundhouse inspecting and repairing steam locomotives. There were often many locomotives in the roundhouse all at once, each standing in its own stall listlessly puffing out its black smoke.

Numerous other smokestacks in the town belched their poisonous fumes further polluting the air. All of this air pollution kept Mother in poor health. Her condition was so acute that a doctor told Dad that if he wanted to keep his wife alive, he must take her to the country.

Dad had been a city boy all his life, first in Nottingham, England, and then in Scranton, so he hadn't the foggiest idea of how to operate a farm. Even so, with such an incentive, he purchased about 50 acres in East Sterling, Pennsylvania. There was no power in the rural areas in those days and water was extracted from a pump a few feet from our house. We had "six rooms and a path." The building at the end of the path was oblong and the plank seat had three large holes and one small one! The outhouses of our neighbors had only one hole. I often wondered why ours had accommodations for so many more occupants!

Dad and Mother worked tirelessly trying to make ends meet, he doing his share of caring for and milking six cows, then walking three or four miles each way to work at a lumber mill. In between he did the plowing, planting, haying and other farm jobs. On the hottest summer days, Mother converted our little frame house into a sauna as she canned wild berries from the woods and vegetables grown in our garden. The process of boiling the Mason jars of food in a large wash boiler atop the wood stove only added to the heat and humidity.

Indeed there was drudgery during my childhood, but there were also times of relaxation and pleasure. Ours was a close-knit family where love was present. Occasionally we would all climb aboard the one-horse buggy to spend an evening with friends who lived two or three miles distant. Steering home by lantern light wasn't a problem as the horse knew the way; in fact, we could have put the buggy on "automatic pilot" except for the downgrades where the buggy threatened to overtake the horse!

I also remember the ornately carved pump organ which sat in the corner of our living room and the beautiful sounds that emanated from it as Mother played. She had a beautiful voice and was frequently invited to sing for various groups in the area. I particularly remember her singing "Whispering Hope," "In the Garden" and "Beautiful Isle of Somewhere," the land for which she would early take her departure.

Saturday night was bath night. Although there was plenty of water in the well, there wasn't much on the stove! After the water had been mixed to the correct temperature in the washtub in the middle of the kitchen floor, my sister Dorothy, who was two years younger than I, had the first go at it. I was next, followed by my mother, and finally my dad. One Saturday night I had two baths. After Mother had helped me dress, I walked too close to the tub, lost my balance—a common thing for me—and ended up back in the tub!

I suppose that the relationship between Dorothy and me was fairly normal for kids. Animosities were strictly an internal matter, and if anyone outside of our family said or did anything to one of us, the other was immediately prepared for battle. Mother would not tolerate overt warfare, so it was necessary for us to find ingenious methods to carry on covert hostility.

In those days it seemed that every mother and

grandmother had aspirations to become a pharmacist. The sulphur and molasses I took in the spring to "thin out the blood" was endurable. But Mother had a concoction for sore throats that really was repulsive—a teaspoonful of kerosene and sugar. By the end of the sore throat season, the mere thought of this cure would cause my stomach to turn. Dorothy's revenge for something I had done to her was often a whisper in my ear, within Mother's hearing, "Kerosene and sugar."

Reading the exploits of cowboys and Indians thrilled me. A friend even made me a miniature bow and arrow set. Mother viewed this piece of military equipment with apprehension but permitted me to keep it. One day, like any proper Indian, I was crouched in the branches of a lilac bush at the corner of the house. Quite by accident, just as I let an arrow fly, Dorothy happened to stroll by the bush. The arrow pricked her cheek only an inch or two from her eye. My pleadings went unheeded as Mother broke my treasure in pieces and put it in the kitchen stove.

From my schoolmates I often heard the expressions "cripple" and "Billy can't do that." I remember being excused from gym classes and being told to read or study in the classroom instead. How embarrassed I felt sitting there alone!

Perhaps one of my worst recollections was Halloween one year. We were all told to bring costumes on the proper day to disguise ourselves. There was a parade with all the kids marching in a big circle. The problem of the limping boy was easily solved. After the first time around, I was pulled out of the parade by a teacher who stood me in front of her and held me by the shoulders. Now the parade was viewed by a half dozen teachers and a scarlet-faced little boy.

During all of my childhood years I had been a consistent bed-wetter. But when I was about nine years old, Mother decided to try an experiment to attempt to break the habit. I think she thought that the promise of a whipping in the morning might cure the problem. Dad had a couple of small-diameter dowel rods from the lumber mill and had them in readiness for the following morning. I was wet as usual.

Mother, being a complete novice in the art of administering a proper spanking, dealt so gentle a stroke that I don't remember any unpleasant sensation, much less actual pain. Even so, by the time the second stroke landed, I had convinced her that unless the experiment was immediately terminated, there would be no remote hope of my surviving more than a few minutes!

I loved my mother dearly, so life took an unpleasant turn when I was 14 and she went to the hospital for surgery. I was later told that the damage done at my birth had made the operation necessary. As was the case of many who were admitted to the hospital in those days, she didn't come out alive.

The bed-wetting problem took on a new significance. In trying to work out a life without Mother, Dad placed Dorothy and me in the home of neighbors for some weeks. It would be so horribly embarrassing to wet their bed! I earnestly pleaded with God that this awful thing would not happen. What a relief the next morning—I was dry! God had heard my pleading and from that time on the problem was over.

We went to school in the village of Newfoundland, Pennsylvania, about a mile and a half from our house in East Sterling. Most of the natives were German immigrants who spoke English with a heavy accent. At that time Dad thought that we should stop attending the tiny Methodist Episcopal church and join the popular Moravian church. So we attended the confirmation classes and were received as members.

All went well until the mailman brought each of us a letter from the church with a bill for membership dues. This was during the Great Depression of the 1930s. My mother's operation and funeral had wiped out the family savings and put us in debt. Dad also had an operation that put him out of work for almost a year. The membership bill was about $24 as I recall, but it may as well have been $2,400. There was no way that we could pay the bill and we were too embarrassed to attend without paying, so we stopped going to Sunday school and church.

During the Prohibiton era, everyone drank on weekends and attended square dances for relaxation after the heavy work week. There were four young men in my gang who, like me, had just finished high school. Each week it was our habit to drive to the home of some European immigrant to buy cheap alcoholic beverages. Many immigrants augmented their meager farm income by producing fiery concoctions for young fellows like us. I remember one woman placing a gallon jug of fire-water into our hands, commenting in broken English, "Look at the little devils in there."

During one square dance, in the process of swinging my partner, I got into reverse and couldn't stop until I had backed through a window and ended up in a heap on the front porch. By the time I picked myself up and staggered back into the house, they were taking up a collection to pay for the broken window.

My body was growing stronger as time went by. Although my right arm and leg were weak, the left side more than made up for it. Many people in our area were felling trees and cutting them into mine props because in the nearby coal mines they were "robbing the pillars"—removing the pillars of coal that supported the ceiling of the mine and replacing them with wooden props. Everyone in the prop business had horses and a few had caterpillar tractors to pull the props to the truck-loading site. One budding businessman couldn't afford a horse so he offered jobs to anyone who would cut the trees down, saw them into the proper lengths and carry them on their shoulders to the loading site. Another young man and I accepted his offer. An eight-hour day of that did quite a bit of body-building! Unknown to me,

God was preparing me for what lay ahead in Irian Jaya.

I was about twenty-one when I met Katie. In my beat-up 1928 Whipett I would drive to her house singing a song I had learned as a kid from my grandparents' Victrola: "K-K-K-Katie, beautiful Katie, you're the only g-g-g-girl that I adore. When the moon shines over the cow shed, I'll be waiting at your k-k-k-kitchen door." She was everything I had ever thought of looking for in a girl. Cupid's darts were penetrating deeply.

The night soon came when I asked her to marry me. She said she would give me her answer after she had time to think it over.

Katie's father was a successful farmer, the undisputed king over his household of wife and 14 children. Even though Katie had passed her 21st birthday, it would have taken some pluck on her part to disobey one of his commands. The night came for Katie to give me her answer. We parked along a lonely country road in my ancient jalopy in a drizzling rain. I urged her to tell me what her decision was. After some hesitation, she gently said, "Bill, I wish that I could say, 'Yes,' but my dad told me, 'Katie, don't marry that guy. He could never support you.'"

My world fell apart. At my feet lay the shattered fragments of my fondest dreams.

3

The Meeting

I WAS DRIVING HOME ALONE ONE NIGHT thinking about my life. It seemed meaningless—working hard, spending my Sundays with a hangover, being both single and lonely. Although I adored babies and little children, I contemplated the possibility that such a dream might never be mine. *If what I have is all that life has to offer,* I thought, *why go on? Why not just end this misery?*

I remembered my boyhood days in the little Methodist Episcopal church before my mother died. I thought of the hymns I had sung so lustily: "I love to tell the story; it did so much for me." I wondered if there was something in the meaning of those words that I was missing.

I stopped my car at the edge of a field, got out and walked a distance into it. As I raised my eyes to gaze at the glory of the starry night, I said, "If there is a God, I would like to find Him." My prayer was very simple, very short, but very earnest. Every earthly thing had resulted in meaninglessness. Could there be meaning in some other-than-earthly experience?

There were no shouts of welcome by the inhabitants of heaven. The celestial spheres continued on their courses just as they had before I spoke. But deep inside of me something changed. I was hungry for God. I sincerely wanted to find Him. "If I'm really seeking God," I reasoned, "the logical thing to do is to go where people say He is." I decided to go to a little Methodist church whose minister I knew and whose daughters had been my schoolmates.

Three Sundays later, the minister approached me: "Bill, the chap who was teaching the young people's Sunday school class quit. Would you be willing to take over in his place?"

One of the first lessons I taught was on temperance—in those days interpreted by the Methodists to mean total abstinence. I said to myself, "If there is one thing I can't stand, it's a hypocrite. If I tell these kids they shouldn't drink, I'll be the first one to quit."

When a Methodist minister in another community gave a two-week seminar on evangelism, I decided to attend. At the end of the sessions he invited those who were willing to follow and serve Christ to come to the altar rail and dedicate their lives to Him. I was among those who did.

By that time I was working in a wood-turning factory where flag staffs were made. The tips, or spearheads as we called them, were turned on a lathe and then drilled by a foot-operated drill press. From a bin full of spearheads at the right side of the drill press, the press operator would take a spearhead between his right thumb and forefinger, place it upside down in a hole in a cast

iron plate and push his foot down. Then pulling
the drilled spearhead out of the hole with his left
hand, would insert the new one with his right. I
think that I broke the speed record by boring 30
or 40 a minute.

One sleepy morning I placed the spearhead in
the hole, put my right forefinger on top of it, and
pushed down with my foot. I was instantly awake!
When I raised my foot, the drill was whirring at
high speed in the second joint of my finger. I slid
the finger down off the drill, turned off the motor,
wrapped a handkerchief around the finger and
drove to the office of the community doctor.

He examined the damage carefully. "You have
cut both tendons, the one that bends the finger
down and the one that pulls it straight again. You
have shattered all the bones in the joint. Your
finger will never again bend at that joint. The only
logical thing to do is to amputate the finger there.
But," he added, "something tells me not to do it.
I will just run a merthiolate swab through it, put
on a splint and see what happens."

At that time I didn't know why he had been so
strongly impressed not to amputate the finger, but
a few years later I realized that a finger which God
has destined to type the New Testament in a
tribal language could never have ended up in a
doctor's wastebasket.

At the next visit I astounded him by bending
the finger at that drilled-out joint. He told me later
that he had reported the incident to a large medical personnel conference. "There is no precedent

in medical history for what you have described,"
they agreed. Not only did the finger work perfectly, but the Master Surgeon had embossed His
signature on the finger with a scar in the shape of
a perfect figure seven.

I continued to seek after God, attending various
special meetings in addition to the services in my
church. Occasionally I was asked to speak, and
became—so I overheard—a model young man.

Meanwhile, I was taking a correspondence
course in mechanical drafting and design. One of
the school's claims was that it would find a job for
its students. I wrote to the school explaining that
I felt ready to take on a job even though I had not
yet graduated. My sister Dorothy was rather
young when she married one of the sons of a
neighbor family. He had studied to become
an electrical engineer and found work in Philadelphia, Pennsylvania. I also hoped to get a job in
that city. The school responded by sending me a
list of company addresses. But I had mixed emo-
tions because God was becoming very important
to me. I wondered if I would continue to walk with
Him if I went to the big city.

By the spring of 1942, the United States was at
war and defense plants were springing up over-
night—"Help Wanted" signs tacked to their
doors. The personnel manager of the first company I interviewed with in Philadelphia kindly
informed me that they were looking for a senior
draftsman with several years of experience. The
second firm, however, was willing to take a young

man standing on the bottom rung of the ladder and help him climb upward.

I immediately began looking for a church to join. The first I visited was a large Methodist one where no one, not even the minister, greeted me. Those hundreds of well-to-do parishioners provided a chilly atmosphere on a hot spring day! The second Sunday, I visited a much smaller Methodist church and felt welcome. It wasn't long until I asked that my letter of membership be transferred from the little country church back home.

One night it seemed that a voice was telling me what an exemplary young man I had become, that I didn't drink, smoke or run around, and was really walking the narrow way. Years later I remembered this incident as I witnessed a Moni custom in Irian Jaya. Warriors slaughter a pig by walking up to it and shooting a "blood valley" arrow into its heart. If the pig is tame and not too big, the executioner doesn't worry too much even if the arrow doesn't go exactly were it should. But if the pig is a large, powerful, half-tamed one, there is the fear that it might become enraged and take off someone's leg before it drops. Consequently, more elaborate preparations are made for its demise. Someone with a long pole and gentle voice approaches the pig and puts food in front of it. Then he begins rubbing the pig's back with the long pole. All this special attention assures the pig that it is in the company of loving friends. It closes its eyes in contentment. The executioner then slowly moves in and takes careful aim. The arrow finds its target and the pig drops dead instantly.

The words I was hearing were like the calming strokes on the back of the pig—but they were from the enemy, the one who I believe knew that Almighty God had planned a special work for this "weak thing."

I was living in Upper Darby, a western suburb of Philadelphia, and had a one-hour daily commute to the defense plant in the northeast part of the city. One day a fellow worker in the engineering department said to me, "Bill, I saw you at church last Sunday, so I assume you must live in the same area that I do. I drive to work. Would you like to ride with me?"

While we rode to work each morning, the radio was invariably tuned to a beautiful program called, "Christian Voices." After a few mornings I said to myself, "These people have something that I don't have. And I want it." Again, going frequently to lonely places to pray, I was full steam in the pursuit of God.

I thought that it was I who was seeking after God, but the truth of the matter was that it was quite the other way—the Divine Guide was constantly just ahead of me, directing each of my steps. Divine omnipotence had protected the "weak thing" from birth and had even managed to build the frail, twisted body into a physically strong and healthy one. And now, divine omniscience was painstakingly providing the right cir-

cumstances to cause me to seek Him at the right
time, a seeking that would eventually take me
halfway around the world.

4

Called

IT WAS A SATURDAY MORNING in August, 1942. I was now 27 years old and living with my sister Dorothy and her family. It was my custom on such mornings to go on long walks with my five-year-old niece. That day I said to her, "Where shall we walk this morning, Barbie?"

"Let's go by my Sunday school," she replied.

Her Sunday school was in a large Presbyterian church. Straight ahead of us on the same side of the street was a Christian Science reading room. And to our left, across the street, was a small, low church building bearing the name "The 69th Street Gospel Tabernacle." It had a large cross raised above it with neon letters proclaiming the message "Jesus Saves."

As I glanced at the church with the elevated cross, a voice said, "Go there." It was neither a shout nor a whisper, but a normal, plain, audible voice spoken very distinctly. I turned around, searching for the source, but Barbie and I were quite alone. I sensed that it was God who had spoken.

The next evening found me inside the church with the long name and the denomination with an even longer name—The Christian and Missionary Alliance. The people in the church with the elevated cross were warm and friendly. They seemed to really love one another and I felt that they loved me, too. *I like these people,* I thought to myself. *I will come back next Sunday evening.*

I returned the third Sunday evening as well. I enjoyed the happy, buoyant songs and choruses. I don't remember what the messages were about; in fact, I wonder if I even heard the message the third Sunday evening because one of the announcements preoccupied my mind. The next day, Labor Day, there was to be a big youth rally in a distant town. Anyone needing transportation was to be in front of the church at 7:30 a.m. All during the service a persistent inner voice urged me to be there.

The Alliance churches which planned the rally had been able to secure the services of a gifted orator, Mrs. Ruth O. Stull, an Alliance missionary to Peru.

The underlying theme of her afternoon message was "full commitment whatever the cost." I remember Mrs. Stull's word picture: God is weaving a tapestry but we are able to see only the back side—the sometimes ugly, meaningless combinations of colors; the broken, spliced threads; the dismal, discouraging picture. But some day we will see the front side with its breathtaking beauty and marvel at the skill of the Master Weaver.

When Mrs. Stull gave the altar call, I went forward to commit myself to the Lord. Again I heard

His voice—not as on the sidewalk two weeks and two days before—but in my inner being, calling me to a full-time ministry which probably would mean foreign service.

The days clicked by. It was Friday evening, and Friday evening was street meeting night. Back home, Holy Rollers did bizarre, outlandish things on the street, but respectable church-goers conducted their services inside church buildings.

I felt ashamed to take an active part in their meeting but reasoned that the least I could do would be to go and stand on the edge of the crowd so as to increase the number of onlookers. So there I was, listening to my new friends exalting Jesus in their testimonies. Then the youth leader, Fred Fowler, shaded his eyes and looked in my direction. "Hey, that's Bill Cutts back there. Bill, how about coming here to the microphone and telling the folks what happened to you last Monday?"

Instantly my reluctance changed into eagerness. I told the people about how empty and meaningless and hopeless my life had once been and how it was full to overflowing since I had received Jesus into my heart.

I can't describe my walk home that night. I certainly had not wanted "to shamelessly take my religion out into the street" as non-Christians termed street meetings, but I had felt God leading me to do what I didn't want to do, and I had obeyed Him. Wave after wave of joy filled my being. I never knew such ecstasy was possible.

On Sunday I told the pastor about my experience. "Bill," he said, "that was the infilling of the Holy Spirit."

I had heard of the Holy Spirit because I had recited the Apostles' Creed many times, but for the first time I heard that the Holy Spirit was willing to live in people. I believed the pastor because I myself knew that something unusual had taken place in my life. On the following Monday morning, I saw my fellow workers through new eyes, eyes of love. I looked for appropriate tracts and stuffed my pockets with them. I couldn't find a tract that I liked for young people, so I wrote one and had it published. I knew what it was to weep over the lost around me.

Jesus said:

> No branch can bear fruit by itself; it must remain in the vine. Neither can you bear fruit unless you remain in me. (John 15:4b)

> I am going to send you what my Father has promised; but stay . . . until you have been clothed with power from on high. (Luke 24:49)

The One who had called the "weak thing" into service for Him was clothing him with His mighty power!

5

The Matchbox

THAT GOD HAD CALLED ME to full-time service I knew for sure. I assumed that meant attending some kind of college, but I was getting older by the minute and most missionary societies had an age limit for overseas candidates.

Which school should I attend? I thought of Prairie Bible Institute in Canada because I was so impressed by the book *Born Crucified*, written by its president, L.E. Maxwell. I took an entrance exam to the Eastern Baptist Theological Seminary and received an acceptance letter. Still, there was no leading from the Lord. Surely I would have direction in time to enter school in the fall of '43, but there was none.

Early in 1944, I became aware of The Missionary Training Institute at Nyack, New York, and by August I boarded a bus for Nyack. The beauty of the place was breathtaking, especially the glory of the sunrise on the Hudson River. Having graduated from high school in 1934, I was 10 years older than most of my fellow students and was therefore given a single room in Wilson Hall, a complex for married couples and single men.

In those days, students were questioned by

their peers as to their future goals in life. If they were not planning to go to the mission field and had no good reason for not going, surely something must be wrong in their relationship with the Lord. I signed up for the theology course, expecting to become a missionary. But I wanted to avoid such embarrassing questions about what a person with my disabilities was doing taking the missions course. I did make sure, however, that I took all of the subjects required for overseas service. I was healthy and strong—that is, my left side was strong—and I would forget that my body appeared different from the bodies of others. As night fell I could see my shadow—a shadow reminiscent of the picture of a gnome in a children's book.

It was during my second year that Satan employed one of his ingenious methods to cause me to deviate from the path God had chosen for me. A couple and their two young children moved into the apartment across the hall. Sally was a beautiful, vivacious, friendly young woman, a joy to be around. Jim was friendly, but reserved, quiet and seemingly deep in thought much of the time. We became close friends.

One day, Jim went to New York City and jumped from the window of a tall building.

Sally and her two children immediately left Nyack. About six months later she sent me a letter recounting how their lives were being slowly put back together. I interpreted her letter as a subtle invitation for me to help them do it.

It wouldn't have been at all difficult to fall in love with Sally. She was everything a young pastor could desire in a helpmeet. I already loved her children and they loved me. I could start out with a delightful, ready-made family. Moreover, I felt that she was too lovely a person to have gotten such a raw deal from life—I could be the noble Sir Galahad, making up for the tragedy this little family had suffered.

Again, there was the inner voice, "No, Bill, I have not called you to a pastor's life, but to take My Word to lost tribespeople in a remote corner of earth."

Had I been free to do what I pleased with my life, I would have immediately answered her letter. But I knew that I was not my own. I was the property of the sovereign God who had called me to do a special work for Him. And I knew that the path along which He was leading me was too narrow to take Sally and her darling children.

The second year at "Dr. Simpson's Matchbox" (so named by its students), I noticed a particular young woman who was always smiling and cheerful. She really loved my Lord and had her sights set on the mission field. We became friends by the end of the year and at graduation time she introduced me to her family. Her name was Grace Betty Silverstein. As I took the summer course and she worked as a deaconess for the Old Stone Church at Nyack, our friendship developed.

I would learn later that Grace Betty's father was a Hebrew Christian and her mother of English descent. The Silversteins had five sons and one daughter, Ruth, who died of tuberculosis just three weeks before Grace Betty's birth. The day Grace Betty was born, her mother read a verse in *Daily Light*: "Take this child and nurse it for me and I will give thee thy wages" (Exodus 2:9 KJV). This daughter, she realized, was only on loan to her. Grace Betty was to belong to God.

On our first date, Grace Betty and I walked to a drugstore, as I had no car during my college years. The expected purchase of some ice cream turned out instead to be a tube of Ergophene, a remedy for a painful sore on her hand. Grace Betty was very appreciative.

My second year, after daring to register without any money, I was offered a job by the business manager. And before it was time to begin the third year, a great-aunt of mine died. No one was prepared for the shock when her will was opened. I was named as her sole heir. In a short time this unexpected inheritance became my possession, not only covering my third-year tuition, but many needs that followed.

One of the names of the sovereign God is Jehovah-jireh, the Lord who provides. He certainly provided in many ways for the needs of this college student.

6

"Marry" Christmas

TOWARD THE END OF MY LAST YEAR at Nyack College, some officials of The Christian and Missionary Alliance came to the campus to interview those of the graduating class who wished to apply for foreign service. I put my name on the schedule.

Not only did I have obvious physical defects, but the Alliance had an age limit of 30 years for first-time missionaries. I would soon be 32. I shared with the examining committee how the Lord had called me to be a missionary on Labor Day, 1942. When I finished, the Personnel Secretary looked me in the eye to make sure that I would get his message: "Mr. Cutts, we wouldn't consider you for foreign service under any circumstances. You have done well here at Nyack. You will be a good pastor, but don't think you could ever become a missionary under The Christian and Missionary Alliance."

But I had information that wasn't yet at his disposal! While I had been waiting for my Lord's leading as to which college to enter, I had attended a missionary convention in our church. One missionary to Indochina poured out his heart, urging young people to come and help him get God's Word into the language and into the hearts of lost mountain people. I was sure that was my Lord's call for me and planned, upon graduation from Nyack, to attend the Wycliffe Summer Institute of Linguistics (SIL) course at Norman, Oklahoma. The experts there could show me how to do the work to which I had been called—translating God's Word into an unwritten language.

Therefore, a short time after graduation, I was on a train to Norman. Not only with books, but also with on-the-job instruction, SIL taught how to decipher a foreign language. An Arapaho woman, one of a large group of North American Indians whom the school brought in, was assigned to me.

I enjoyed working with her despite her extreme frankness. One day I asked her for an expression in her language and she replied, "I told you that yesterday. You will never be able to learn my language."

The course taught us how to approach a language on a monolingual basis—gathering material directly from the informant with no common language used for asking questions. After stacks of material had been gathered, we were told to analyze it, write a grammar describing the language, make up primers for teaching people to read, and finally produce readers to give them lots of practice.

At the end of that gruelling summer in Oklahoma's unbelievable heat, Dr. Eugene Nida approached me. "You did a good job here this summer, Bill. What are you going to do with your life?"

I replied, "I feel that the Lord Himself called me into The Christian and Missionary Alliance, but they turned me down flat. Maybe if you tell them what you just told me they might change their minds."

"I'll do that, Bill," he promised.

After finishing the summer course, I wrote to the Home Secretary of the Alliance telling him that I was ready to go to work. He sent my letter to the superintendent of the Western District. A response was not long in coming. I was instructed to candidate in a little independent church in Newton, Iowa.

I was met at the bus station and taken to the home of an elderly spinster, Miss Hermea Murphy. The plan was that, following supper, the congregation would listen to this young chap fresh out of college, decide whether or not to keep him, and if so, work with him to draw up a contract. So it was that I became the pastor of the Newton church.

Miss Murphy was about 70 years old, one of the pillars of the little church and a truly unique individual. She was kind and generous, but she had an inflexible code of ethics. If a thing was right, she was for it and there were no deviations. No one needed to guess where she stood on a given issue. She said exactly what she thought and was a real stickler for punctuality.

One evening I was sitting on the platform ready to begin the meeting. The congregation consisted only of Miss Murphy. At the exact hour for the meeting, she announced: "It's seven o'clock—time to start."

I replied, "Nobody is here yet."

"We're here!" she responded.

The meeting began at the scheduled time with an acapella duet. I realized that my textbooks at Nyack hadn't taught me all that I should know about pastoring a church and early came to respect her judgment on many issues.

Miss Murphy was a living example of frugality. While I was at Newton, the city officials inaugurated a garbage pickup and disposal system. Contributions were requested from the population in order to pay for it. When the collectors arrived at Miss Murphy's door their request for a donation was unsuccessful. "How do you intend to dispose of your garbage?" they asked her.

"I eat my garbage," she replied.

Miss Murphy offered to loan me all sorts of things to make the parsonage livable. I certainly needed all the help I could get for I had arrived in Newton with little more than a suitcase. The day came when I owned a counterpart for each of the items she loaned me and I borrowed a car to return hers. "Well," she remarked, "you're the first preacher I ever knew to bring anything back that he borrowed."

Later on, after I was married, I was urging the congregation to vote to become a full-fledged Alliance church by extolling the advantages it would bring. In my best rhetoric I cried, "My first loyalty is to my Lord Jesus Christ. My second is to The Christian and Missionary Alliance. At this point, Miss Murphy turned to my wife and in a stage-whisper asked, "Where do you come in?"

After her graduation from Nyack, Grace Betty had gone to Kentucky to fulfill the one-year home service requirement before going overseas. Now she was back home in New York state serving as a deaconess in her uncle's church at Albany.

I was finding the tiny parsonage at Newton very large and very lonely and began writing to her frequently. One letter audaciously pled: "If you will join me in the Lord's work, you will increase my efficiency one thousand percent because the Word states: 'One shall chase a thousand, two put ten to flight.' "

Grace Betty responded dutifully by going directly to New York City to talk to the godly A.C. Snead, Foreign Secretary of the Alliance. "Dr. Snead, I have a problem. A young man has asked me to marry him and I am a candidate preparing to go to the mission field under the Alliance. What must I do?"

Dr. Snead didn't believe in single missionaries, so he asked Grace Betty, "Did your young man ever apply for foreign service?"

"Yes," she replied, "I'm sure that he must have."

A search was made for my application. They found none—because I had been rejected so emphatically I thought it a waste of time and postage to mail in a written application. But what they did find was a letter from my promise-keeping friend, Dr. Eugene Nida of SIL, saying in effect, "If you don't want him, we do."

Dr. Snead encouraged Grace Betty to continue with her engagement, saying, "Tell your young man to send us a written application."

So it was that an ordinary October day turned into a red-letter day when the Alliance pastor at Newton received a telegram bearing the message: "Dr. Snead pronounces his blessing. Marry Christmas."

The wedding was on December 20, 1947. The bride's father provided friends and relatives with a lovely banquet and the new bride and groom with a round-trip rail ticket for a mini honeymoon.

I sent an application for foreign service to the Alliance headquarters and in due time received word that we had been accepted, provided that I could pass a physical exam.

A doctor glanced at Grace Betty and asked her if she wanted to go overseas. When she said that she did, her examination was over. She was written up as being physically fit.

I was dealt with in similar fashion by another doctor. He merely sat at his desk and filled out the form. When he had finished, I asked him, "Well, did you pass me?"

"Certainly not!"

"On what basis?"

"On the basis that the army didn't accept you for military service."

We were stopped dead in our tracks a second time!

But we were the bondslaves of the One who opens doors that no man can shut. I knew that the One who had called me into His service on Labor Day 1942 had the power to turn that red light green.

Back in my study, I wrote the Society headquarters and described my make-believe physical examination. I felt I had been given a raw deal. They felt the same way and requested that I be examined by Dr. V.S. Barkey who was a member of the Omaha Alliance Church. They expressed full confidence in his abilty and judgment and said his word would be final.

Dr. Barkey gave me a thorough examination and decided that I had a perfectly healthy, strong, albeit bent-out-of-shape body.

How ludicrous, how futile for humans to work so hard to close a door being held open by the sovereign God!

7

Irian Jaya

IN A VERY SHORT TIME we received word from headquarters that we had been accepted for foreign service. Grace Betty had her sights set on Africa; I had originally applied to go to French Indochina to do Bible translation work among the mountain tribespeople. Now the question became: "Would you consider an appointment to Dutch New Guinea?"

In the early 1600s, the Dutch displaced the Portugese who were the first to establish themselves in Indonesia. During the Second World War, the Japanese captured Indonesia, but three days after their surrender to the United States, a group of nationalists proclaimed independence. In 1949, the Netherlands ceded independence to the Republic of Indonesia, retaining control of only Dutch New Guinea. After several years of fighting, Dutch New Guinea also became a part of Indonesia in 1963. It is now called Irian Jaya. The Alliance first went to Indonesia in 1928. Missionaries were the first white people to enter the interior of Irian Jaya. Because of its relative isolation and other historical and political factors, Irian

Jaya is administered as a separate field by The
Christian and Missionary Alliance.

About the 15th of December in Brooklyn, New
York, we boarded Isthmian Line's beautiful new
freighter, the SS *Steelworker*. The trip was like flip-
ping, page-by-page, through an exotic travel
book. The Panama Canal! Honolulu! Bangkok!
Viet Nam! We arrived in Surabaya, Java, after sailing on the *Steelworker* for two and a half months.
Two more weeks of sea travel were still ahead of
us.

Our first night in the local hotel found numerous mosquitoes trying to occupy our space.
About midnight I set out in search of some repel-
lant. I had been studying Malay from a little book
someone had given to me when we sailed. Now
was the opportune time to find out just how prof-
itable my weeks of study had been. I found a man
in the kitchen and put together my little statement: "I request medicine to make dead mosquitoes." The man listened to my utterance several more times, then called another. They both
listened carefully, then called another and another until I had enough of an audience for a
small church service. Finally one of them got the
message and brightly announced to his fellows,
"*Beliau minta* FLIT"—Mister requests FLIT. FLIT
was the internationally known name for a popular
insecticide. I had passed my first foreign language
encounter!

The final two weeks of our lovely voyage behind
us, we were warmly greeted by Alliance mission-

aries at the seaport of Makassar. We had arrived!

Before the foundation of the world, the eternal, omnipotent, omniscient God had planned to make a missionary out of the "weak thing." Men in places of authority had said, "Unthinkable." But our God is sovereign. He had other plans.

8

An Angel in High Places

MAKASSAR—NOW UJUNG PANDANG—WAS The Christian and Missionary Alliance headquarters for the field of Indonesia and was also the site of the Bible school. Grace Betty and I were immediately assigned to language study for eight hours a day. Mr. and Mrs. Tetelepta, Indonesian students at the Bible School, were appointed to be our teachers. Mr. Tetelepta was to be my teacher, and his wife would teach Grace Betty. I was very grateful that it wasn't the other way around for Mrs. Tetelepta talked like a machine gun.

One day for some reason, Mrs. Tetelepta was my informant. It was a frustrating experience. I could see the newspaper headlines screaming: "Missionary Clubs Teacher With Chair." But Grace Betty liked her as much as I liked her husband. Many years later, prior to our final return to America, we were with this now elderly couple for a short visit. True to her inherent love for teaching, Mrs. T was still correcting my mistakes in Indonesian!

After five months at the mission guest home in Makassar we contacted the field chairman. "Mr. Brill, we've learned enough Indonesian to be able to talk to people, so do you have some station where we can work and continue our language study at the same time?"

"I'd like you to go to the island of Sumbawa," he responded, "and help the three national pastors we have there." Sumbawa Island was nearly 100 percent Muslim. "I have written two letters to the sultan asking permission for you to go there, but he has not responded. What do you think of my just putting you on a boat and waiting to see what happens?"

This arrangement certainly held the promise of an interesting arrival! Trusting our Lord for His enabling, we set sail. What a joyous meeting with the three pastors, their wives and a few others who had assembled to meet the ship. We were taken to a lovely inn operated by the government. The local pastor accompanied us to all the necessary offices, one of which was the office of the sultan's secretary, where we applied for a house. We were given the other half of the duplex in which Pastor Taka and his family lived.

One of the items in our outfit was a shortwave radio that could pull in stations from great distances. Today, such radios run on flashlight batteries. But in 1949, the transistor was yet to be invented, so powerful radios were full of tubes which guzzled an enormous amount of electricity. To run the radio, we brought along an automobile battery. We also brought a windcharger because we knew that there would be no source of electricity to charge the battery in interior New Guinea.

A windcharger has a short frame with a propeller at one end and a tail at the other to make it face into the wind at all times. A small generator is mounted at the back, and as the propeller rotates, the generator also turns, charging the battery connected to it. The completed assembly weighs about 35 pounds and mounts on a solid platform above any surrounding objects that would cut off the wind.

I explained this to Mr. Taka on the way to the office of the Department of Forestry. An official listened to my story and promised to help.

A few days later a truck stopped in front of our yard and dropped off four poles about 40 feet in length. I managed to raise them to form a tower with four sides and braced it well. The next step was to assemble the little aluminum tower that was packed with the windcharger and bolt it to the tiny platform on top of my wooden tower.

The aluminum tower had at its top a spindle that was designed to fit into a bearing hole at the bottom of the windcharger frame. The spindle was about six feet above the wooden platform, a bit higher than my eye level. It was necessary to run wires from the unit to the battery via a circuit breaker and an ammeter.

The final operation in the assembly was to tie a rope to the windcharger, hoist it up to the platform, grasp it with two hands, raise it above one's head, match up the bearing hole with the spindle and lower the unit into position.

So there I was standing 35 feet above the ground on the tiny platform with no railing, with the windcharger resting in my outstretched hands. I have never had a good sense of balance, and this occasion was no exception. I felt myself leaning over backwards. At that point I could have done what any sensible person would have done—drop the windcharger and grab the aluminum tower. But I had only one windcharger and was so intent on finishing the job that such a remedy never occurred to me. As I leaned farther and farther back, the angle became more obtuse. I was headed for the ground far below with the windcharger still resting in my outspread hands. I wondered how Grace Betty would get on without me.

Suddenly I felt a hand on the back of each shoulder. The hands pushed me back up into an upright position. I lined up the bearing hole and the spindle, lowered the unit into place and climbed down the ladder.

God's plan for the "weak thing" was not finished yet.

9

The Pillar Moves

IN THE FALL OF 1950, the government of the Netherlands informed our mission that they would permit two more missionaries to enter New Guinea. Our promised land was open. Like the ancient Israelites, loaded down with herds and flocks and the spoils of Egypt, we repacked our outfit and set out.

We got our papers in Makassar and then took a Royal Shipping Line vessel to New Guinea. We arrived in the wee hours of the morning, anchored out at sea and waited for daylight when we could tie up to the pier. As the anchor was dropped, a shudder ran through the ship. Startled from her sleep, Grace Betty asked, "Bill, what's that?"

I replied, "There's nothing to worry about. The helmsman just reversed the propeller to slow down."

I was amused at her calm, matter-of-fact, totally-committed-to-whatever-fate-might-bring statement, "No, Bill, this ship is sinking!"

After a night or two in port, we boarded a plane for Biak Island. Biak was to be our point of departure for interior New Guinea. We were there several weeks, first waiting for our outfit drums to catch up with us, then sorting supplies, which we marked in priority fashion to be shipped when needed.

Eventually we were advised by the Royal Dutch Navy that they were ready to fly us into the Wissel Lakes. The planes they used were PBYs— World War 2 amphibians that took off from the Biak air field and landed on the water at the lakeside village of Enarotali. Passengers sat in the gun turret which had a big plexiglas blister on each side, affording an excellent view in every direction. Over an hour later the flying boat landed on Paniai, the largest of the three Wissel Lakes.

A canoe came to pick us up. Suddenly, as though we had stepped into a time machine that sped us back through centuries of civilization to the Stone Age, we were in the "land that time forgot." We had read nothing about New Guinea and had seen no pictures. What a shock when the canoe pulled alongside the little pier upon which a score of men were standing, clad only in gourds!

There were four missionaries in Enarotali to greet us: Ken and Vida Troutman, and two women—Mary McIlrath, who was involved in a teaching ministry, and Marion Doble who was translating the Bible into Ekari, the language of the Wissel Lakes area. Only four other missionaries were assigned to New Guinea: the Einar Mickelsons who were on furlough and the Gerry Roses out on the coast.

When Grace Betty and I arrived in Enarotali, we

found that a tribe (the Monis) and a house (in Homeyo), had already been picked out for us. We would proceed there as soon as we could get our gear ready and as soon as 40 carriers could be assembled to escort us.

It was while we were waiting to move that our Lord performed another miracle. A Bible school had been started at Enarotali to train Ekari pastors who came from all over the Wissel Lakes region. Some of them were from the Kebo area directly across the lake. Because of high water and the trails being flooded, it would take them a couple of days to walk home around the lake. Wouldn't it be easier if the missionary would be their "father" and take them home in his boat with the outboard motor? (All male missionaries in that section of the island are called "father" and their wives "mama.")

"Bill, did you ever run a boat with an outboard motor?" Ken Troutman queried.

"Never."

"Well, it's just like driving a car. You pull the rope to start the motor. When the boat starts heading in some direction other than what you want, you just pull the handle to the right or to the left to compensate. Would you like to give it a try?"

"Sure, I'm game," I replied.

It was a beautiful morning with a vivid blue sky, the sun occasionally ducking behind fleecy white clouds. Ken had loaded sufficient fuel for the trip. The students and Grace Betty piled in. I pulled the rope. The motor cheerfully responded. Out in the main body of water, there were little waves, just enough to produce a gentle slap, slap under the bow.

At Kebo the boatload of students disembarked. In unison everyone gratefully shouted, "*Koyaa!*" (thank you and good-bye) and we got back into the boat.

Within a few moments we rounded the hook shutting distant Kebo out of our view. The sun was disappearing behind a gray overcast and the wind was increasing. The slap, slap under the bow now became more audible as the motor pushed us laboriously through the mounting waves. We had been advised, "Never go out on the lake without heavy jackets." Now, thankful for the advice, we put them on.

Suddenly the motor stalled. I pulled the starter rope again and again. Yes, there was plenty of fuel in the tank. No, the spark plug was not fouled. The national accompanying us also pulled the rope, but the motor refused to catch. Time passed. The sky grew darker. We looked toward the shoreline—it was receding. The wind was slowly but inexorably pushing us out toward the middle of the lake.

In that area of the world darkness descends a few minutes past six. If darkness fell while we were drifting in the middle of the lake, there would be no hope of our being found before daylight. It's unbelievable how quickly one gets chilled to the bone at 6,000 feet altitude with no sun and surrounded by water. It would be a miserable night under the best of circumstances. But if a heavy rain came up and poured down into the open boat, soaking the passengers. . . . Or if a big wind arose, churning the surface of the lake into huge waves. . . .

"Dear Lord, the one whom You called is in a fix!"

We stopped pulling the rope and the three of us bowed our heads, asking the Lord to come to our rescue. The national was either a Christian or fast becoming one! We prayed for perhaps 10 minutes. Then I stood up and pulled the starting rope. That motor's hum was the most beautiful music we ever heard. Within feet of the shore the motor sputtered and died, but our helper quickly paddled us alongside the pier.

The next morning Ken opened up the motor and inspected the tank. He found no gasoline— only half a tankful of water. Had the sovereign God, who long ago turned water into wine, now reached into the heart of primitive Dutch New Guinea and turned our water into gasoline?

10

Homeyo

ABOUT THE MIDDLE OF DECEMBER 1950, Ken told us that the way was now open for us to move east. A native war had been going on in the area of Homeyo, but it had simmered down—as much as a war could simmer down in Moni land at that time. Ken got the largest dugout canoe owned by the mission and brought it alongside the pier. As nationals carried our supplies down to the lake, he stowed our gear carefully aboard in order to keep the boat in balance. There was just enough space for Grace Betty and me to sit in the middle of the boat and for him to sit at the stern directly in front of the big outboard motor.

We were soon headed across the lake and up the river to the village of Komapa. The trip was treacherous and required the constant attention of our skilled boatman. Submerged logs and huge tree branches shared the river with us. Hitting one of them could easily upset the boat, spilling its contents into the water. Occasionally a propeller pin sheared off as the prop struck a submerged object. While it was being replaced, we drifted at the mercy of the current, but after nearly four hours on the river we arrived at the large Ekari village of Komapa, where Ken had built a trail house.

We were up about five, eating breakfast, putting on our trail boots and replacing the gear in its proper containers for the journey. We distributed the loads to the carriers and at about six o'clock, with barely enough light to see the trail, we were on our way. The first few hours we trekked in the flatlands of the Paniai basin. The trail led through swampland—large areas consisting of about two feet of soft, black mud resting on a foundation of semi-solid ground. The mud in turn was covered with a layer of low, flat vegetation giving it the appearance of a mowed field. I had no difficulty with this morass. I would stand on each little rise of ground which surrounded the mud holes, as if waiting for a starting gun, then make the 50-or-so-yard dash to the next rise.

But poor Grace Betty! Time after time she would break through the ground-vine layer and sink into the mud above her knees. From my vantage point on the rises, it looked like a football game with the "ball" travelling a little distance, getting stopped dead, and then being surrounded by a group of carriers who lifted it into position for the next "kickoff." Adding to her embarrassment, when the carriers were just ready to lift her up, I would yell, "Hold it right there, Grace Betty, until I get a picture!"

Eventually we were at the base of the mountain over which the trail led. The trail between

Enarotali and Homeyo was well travelled by the nationals and could actually be pleasant if it was not raining. However, it was hard work going up, up, up and equally hard going down, down, down the other side before coming to the next up, up, up. Parts of the terrain were so rugged that for long distances the trail would be a stream bed and we often had to climb over or detour around large fallen trees.

Where the rivers were swollen, the tribesmen built bridges consisting of several thick strands of vine usually with circlets of smaller vines attached to them to form the approximately six-inch-wide footpath. Along each side, at about the height of an average person's armpit, was another cable made of several strands of thick vine. Finally there were many, many strands of smaller vines or split vines (they split them with their teeth) tied between each handrail and the footpath. The cross-section of a bridge looked like a large V with about three feet distance between the two handrails.

Many people have lost their lives falling off these bridges. My personal attitude was that if such a bridge was necessary to do my Lord's work, I could trust Him for safety. A missionary prays most fervently while watching one of his children cross a bridge seated on the shoulders of a carrier. Even though tons of missionary baggage have travelled this route, I know of no instance where a missionary lost even one piece of equipment as it made the crossing.

While we were waiting at Enarotali, someone had given us a small puppy that became part of the caravan to our new home in the east. It rode in a carrying-net most of the time, but as we came to the bridge, I nestled it under my right arm. Hanging onto the handrail with only my left hand, I started across the bridge with the puppy. I was wearing heavy, leather, spiked boots and one of them slid off the footpath. What a predicament! I couldn't get my foot and leg back up on the bridge with only one free arm and there was no place to set the puppy down.

A carrier who knew Indonesian saw my predicament, placed his load on the ground at the end of the bridge and hurried to my side. When we reached the shore he proceeded to give me a good tongue-lashing. "You were willing to lay down your life for this worthless dog and thus keep the Monis from hearing the gospel!" I realized that, despite my carelessness, my sovereign Lord had once again preserved my life. Perhaps He was talking to me through the lips of that uneducated Ekari.

In order to make sure that we wouldn't get left behind on the trail, missionaries always travelled at the center of the national escort, some of the carriers leading the expedition and others bringing up the rear. One day, I found a piece of our luggage sitting in the middle of the path. My heart sank, for I had read about expeditions where carriers abandoned their loads and just melted into the bush. I yelled. A carrier approached. "Don't get shook up (loose translation!), Tuan. The man who was carrying that load broke his gourd, and being embarrassed that your wife might see him without proper attire, he ducked into the bush to put on a new one."

There were brief rest stops along the way, some of them in high mountain passes where the extreme cold urged us to keep moving. These stops, with hot coffee and cookies, gave zest to our lagging spirits, not to mention our weary bodies.

At the first stop we got out a box of cookies that our Enarotali hostess had packed for us. Grace Betty noticed the hungry looks in the faces of our carriers. She offered each carrier a cookie out of the tin, pleased that there were enough to go around. One of the carriers had been somebody's houseboy and had previously been introduced to the cookie, but the others were fresh out of the woods. Each took a nibble from his cookie, made a wry face, and gave it to the former houseboy. What a waste of cookies!

Ken was certainly a godsend on this trek with these rookie missionaries. He knew just the places where we should stop for the night—terrain suitable for pitching our tents, a little mountain stream for cooking, filling canteens and washing up; proper materials for the carriers to build themselves a large lean-to; and lots of dry firewood for all of us. He hoped to get to the campsite by about 2:00 p.m. to beat the late afternoon rains. On later trips we would learn how miserable it can be to have the rain arrive first and to go to bed in wet sleeping gear without a cooked supper.

Ken was also the chef, and an excellent one. "Today's Special" was boiled rice, a can or two of corned beef, and a can or two of soup. Dessert would be tinned Dutch candy or cookies.

One night, not far from the campsite, I saw an eerie, ethereal light glowing a few feet ahead of me. My flashlight revealed some pieces of rotting wood. I switched off the light and still there before me was the luminescent pile. In my youth I had read about fox-fire but was never quite convinced that it really existed. Now, in boyish fashion, I struggled back to the tent with a big piece of the rotting wood, planning to crawl back into my sleeping bag, turn off the flashlight, poke Grace Betty and give her a good scare. She wouldn't wake up! At 5:00 a.m. when I lighted our lantern and she came to, she sleepily asked, "Bill, why on earth did you bring that big piece of wood into the tent?"

Dawn's early light found us breakfasted, packed and on our way to another seemingly endless eight-hour workout before our trail guide would say, "Here we are!" The second day ended and again, the carriers built their lean-to and gathered firewood. Again Ken set up his tent and helped us set up ours. Again he unpacked the kettles and cooked "Today's Special." Everything was the same as it had been the night before except that tonight our muscles hurt more and there were more and bigger blisters on our feet.

The third morning began at five as the other two had; every moving part of our bodies screamed to be still. We pulled thick, cold, wet trail socks over blistered feet and heavy wet trail boots over them, wondering if the agony that accompanied the first step of the day would continue to step number ten thousand or step number twenty thousand. We dreamed of having a hot shower and sleeping in a real bed in a real house again.

About noon we broke out of the woods at the summit of a hill that was denuded by the Moni agricultural system of slash, burn, plant, harvest, go to another section of forest, slash, burn. . . . Ken told us that the distant village was Homeyo and that another hour of walking would find us in his little house.

The "weak thing" was standing in Moni land at last, the place where, long before, the sovereign God had called him to be.

"He gives strength to the weary/ and increases the power of the weak./ Even youths grow tired and weary,/ and young men stumble and fall;/ but those who hope in the Lord/ will renew their strength./ They will soar on wings like eagles;/ they will run and not grow weary,/ they will walk and not be faint" (Isaiah 40:29–31).

11

Moni Hazi

SOME HAVE ASKED, "Why do you go and bother those whom you call heathen? They have their religion and it doesn't matter what a person believes so long as he or she is sincere."

Indeed the Monis did have their religion. And they were sincere. But what a religion! When we went to them, they had a concept of a mighty being way off somewhere who was totally apathetic to the needs of people. His name was Emo Zu. The first part of his name is also the Moni word for atmosphere or weather. I never was able to figure out whether the two words were merely homophones with no relationship to each other, or whether there was some connection between Emo Zu and weather.

Dying people were urged to confess their sins to Emo Zu, but Emo Zu couldn't care less about what happened to them. What did concern the Monis, however, was how the evil spirits regarded them. It was hoped, though never proven, that there could be peaceful coexistence with the evil spirits if one went to a lot of bother to appease them. The Monis' garden fences had wide, flat "roofs" on them to keep the rain from rotting the wood underneath. On these roofs they offered food to the spirits in the hope that they wouldn't bother the garden. A common practice among the people was to set aside a portion of each garden for the spirits. It would be carefully tended, but no one would think of eating anything out of that dedicated section.

Sickness was attributed to an evil spirit's anger about something. For example, the Moni name for pneumonia is "devil's arrow." Their name for the awful, leprosy-like skin disease yaws—incurable before the missionaries went there with drugs—is "devil's wound." Pigs would be killed in the name of the spirit believed responsible for the person's illness in the hope that the evil spirit would leave his or her body and the person would be well again.

It was felt that the local evil spirits, although 100 percent rascals, weren't beyond appeasement if the people worked at it. But sometimes there would be an epidemic in which a number of people died, and in such cases it was assumed that a whole contingent of evil spirits from another area had moved in. There would be no hope of placating a gang like that, so the whole village would pick up and flee the region, leaving their houses intact. Coming upon such a deserted site, a traveler might at first think that it was a normal village with everyone gone for the day. Closer inspection revealed hearths that had long ago become cold and weeds growing up in village paths. These are the conditions that greeted Gracie and me.

Moni babies are given names with meaning, such as "Arrow of the People on the Other Bank." But parents often felt that if they gave their child a horrible name, the evil spirits would think that they didn't love the child and would therefore let it alone.

On our first furlough, I was telling a teacher at the Summer Institute of Linguistics about Moni names and asked him to guess why a certain Moni was offended when I addressed him as "Dog Feces." Imagine the teacher's astonishment when I told him that my breach of etiquette lay not in the inference of such a name, but in the fact that I had the wrong animal! The Moni's name was "Pig Feces!" With pigs occupying such a predominant place in their society, this was not at all offensive. It is understandable, then, that when Monis become Christians, they usually take on a new name, a Bible name or the name of a missionary. Similarly, though not for the same reason, my wife's name changed in each of her new environments. She was christened Grace Betty. At Nyack College she was known as GB. When she arrived in New Guinea, she became Gracie.

The people thought that Gracie and I were evil spirits, and presumably evil spirits in corporeal form are more of a hazard than invisible or semi-invisible ones. Their reasoning went something like this: the people of New Guinea are of the black race (though their skin is actually brown).

Most had never seen anything but black people, so they assumed that everyone in the world was black. In order to account for us they explained, "These black people"—referring to Gracie and me—"lived long ago. They died and were buried. In the ground they bleached out. They came back to life. Anything that comes back from the dead is an evil spirit." I believe that God used their fear of us to preserve our lives more than once.

One day a large group of fully armed men came to our yard. I knew nothing of the language and was trying to jot down on paper the few isolated utterances that I could make out. The final speaker was the old chief, Kiguabi. After his speech, everyone stood up and walked away.

About a year later I was working with my informant. Zeoni Mala, "Arrow of the People on the Other Bank," was a clever young man and fun to work with. At coffee break, Zeoni said, "Tuani, do you remember that time when a large group of armed men came into your yard and after Kiguabi got up and made a speech, they all went home?"

"Yes, I remember," I replied.

"Do you know what they came for?"

"I haven't the foggiest idea (another loose translation)!"

"Well, they came to kill you and Mama. That day was the day when my family was laying out the cowrie shells to purchase my wife. But I skipped the ceremony, thinking that it would be more interesting to go down to your house and watch you get killed. This is the speech that old

Kiguabi made that day: 'Friends, let's carefully consider what we are about to do. You know that generations ago our forefathers handed down a prophecy which said that some day *hazi* would come to the Monis out of the west.' " *Hazi* means something wonderful, something permanent, something for which everyone longs. The concept runs through the whole New Guinea island.

"Our forefathers prophesied: '*Hazi* will some day come out of the west. It won't come in our day. It may not come in our children's day. But some day *hazi* will come to the Monis. Blessed is the generation to whom it comes. They must be sure to receive it.' Friends, these people," pointing to Gracie and me, "have come here out of the west. Perhaps they are bringing the *hazi* for which our forefathers told us to wait and to receive when it comes. Let's not kill them. Let's wait and see what happens."

Tears run down my face as I write this. Our God, long before He called us to New Guinea, had put into the hearts of those people a revelation so plain and so forceful that generation after generation, they would recount to their children the prophecy that had been revealed to them. Then, just as the warriors were fingering their arrows that day, God caused Kiguabi to remind them of that old prophecy.

Truly, "The angel of the Lord encamps around those who fear him,/ and he delivers them./ Taste and see that the Lord is good;/ blessed is the man who takes refuge in him" (Psalm 34:7–8).

12

Alice Hope

GRACIE AND I SPENT OUR SATURDAYS trekking to villages and inviting people to come to Homeyo the next day to hear about the Chief of the Sky. We wanted to tell them how He loved people so much that He sent His Son to this earth to die for them, and how those who "take the mind of Jesus" become the children of the Chief of Heaven and live forever and ever.

Once we hiked an hour or more to a village only to find no one in it. We decided to wait until they returned from their gardens or from wherever they had gone. As we waited, we heard murmurings from behind the bushes and houses. The whole village was there, but hidden, afraid to have us see them. How could we reach such a people?

God was soon to make a way. A young Moni woman died. Because of the good rapport we had with Kiguabi, we were invited to attend the funeral. It was decided that Gracie would go.

"Did the woman have any children?" she asked.

"Yes," they said, "that's her baby," pointing to a girl about five months old, barely able to sit up.

"What will happen to the baby?"

61

Their looks of amazement at Gracie's question indicated that they considered it a stupid one. "She will die; what else?" they answered.

Gracie learned that the Moni custom forbade a nursing woman to share her milk on a permanent basis with a baby other than her own. We have seen a woman with a baby on one breast and a baby pig on the other because her husband would probably beat her insensible if the pig died. But there was no milk available for a baby in Moni land if its mother died.

The baby's father was cutting up funeral pork. When a person becomes ill, pigs are sacrificed in the name of the evil spirit believed responsible. Then when the person departs this life, more pigs are sacrificed. The Monis believe that when one dies, he or she goes down into the ground to an existence of total misery that can be alleviated somewhat by sending pork down to him or her so that he or she won't be hungry in addition to his or her other woes. Sending pigs to the deceased is also a safety precaution. The dead, upon their demise from this life, take on new powers. If one is down there hungry, he or she just might begin thinking of all his or her relatives and friends in the other world happily eating pork and become upset. The dead person might come back, kill a lot of pigs and people and make life generally unbearable for them. So their version of bringing flowers to a grave is not only an expression of love, but also cheap insurance against potential misfortune.

Nearby, a hut was full of people with mud smeared on their faces and bodies. Each woman or girl from toddler age upward had a finger newly amputated at the first joint. Their wailing continued on and on, hour after hour: "O my daughter, where have you gone? Why did you leave us? Who will care for your newborn little one? O, our daughter, are you suffering? Are you cold? Are you in anguish? O my little bird! O my little bird!"

In First Thessalonians 4:13, Paul tells those believers: "Brothers, we do not want you to be ignorant about those who fall asleep, or to grieve like the rest of men, who have no hope." Some of the others who "have no hope" are the Monis. For them, the death of a loved one is final, total separation forever and ever.

As the tiny baby's father continued cutting up the pork, Gracie asked, "May I take your baby home with me?"

"Okay, go ahead," he replied.

She wondered if the new widower had understood her question. "Are you sure that I may take your baby with me?"

"That's fine, and here's a piece of pork for you to take along with her."

Gracie arrived home with a Moni net hanging down her back suspended by a headband. Moni nets are made with a large, loose weave making it obvious what is being carried in them.

"What do you have there, Gracie?" I asked.

"It's a baby."

"I can see that it's a baby. Whose baby?"

"It's our baby," she replied.

That was my introduction to Alice Hope. We named her Alice because we thought she would be having an *Alice in Wonderland* experience living with us, Hope because we hoped that if we raised her, she would some day become a great blessing to her own people.

Getting Alice was a sudden, unexpected development to say the least. No layette awaited the arrival of our new baby, but there were always the disposable diapers used by the native women—large leaves with a non-shiny, semiabsorbent surface on one side. Gracie went out to gather a day's supply of what she thought was the right thing. Poor baby Alice in Wonderland! Her first diapers in the home of those strange white people were nettles! A large stack of embroidered tea towels were quickly exchanged for the disposable diapers!

People kept coming to our house expecting to see the little one more and more emaciated and finally departing this life as all motherless babies had done since the beginning of Moni time. Their amazement knew no end when they saw a fat, smiling little one dressed in a beautiful "foreign net."

It wasn't necessary for us to tell the people that we loved them. Right before their eyes was a demonstration which spoke more eloquently than words ever could. "These white foreigners obviously love our baby, and in raising her, are doing for her—one not their own—what we never thought of doing for our very own. Is it possible that they are not evil spirits after all? Is it possible that they are people just as we are, only with skin of a different color?''

The news of the Moni baby thriving in the foreigners' home spread throughout the area. Now when we went to a village, we were received by smiling people. People wanted to hear about our Chief of the Sky and came to the services in the crudely-built little church at Homeyo.

What an array of keys hangs from the waist of the One who opens doors that no one can shut! He has the right key for every locked door on earth.

13

Kill Those Evil Spirits

" **M**AYBE THEY'RE NOT EVIL SPIRITS; maybe
they're people!" The possibility of
this statement being true quickly
encouraged other widowers to take advantage of
the new nursery services. In rapid succession we
acquired a total of four babies. Dear, godly, gentle
Dr. Snead, Foreign Secretary of The Christian and
Missionary Alliance wrote to us, reminding us
that the policy of the Alliance is to evangelize the
lost rather than to start orphanages! Then, to
soften any pain that statement might have
caused, his closing line read: "I hope that in your
ministry to the Monis, it won't be necessary for
you to take in too many more babies."

A little Baptist church in the States heard about
our new family and pledged themselves to send
us 30 dollars per month so that we could bring a
girl from the coast to be the babies' housemother
and pay her wages. We constructed a little building near our house and made arrangements for
Dina to come. She faithfully tended the babies
and did everything she could to please us.

Many of our neighbors, however, were still
questioning whether or not we were really evil

spirits. One day a delegation came to our door announcing, "We know that you are not evil spirits but are truly people. However, in order for us to go back to the doubters and convince them, we are asking you to take us on a tour of your house. People are saying that the spirits of the orphans' dead mothers are under your bed and to feed a baby, you just push it beside its mother's spirit when it cries for food. They are saying that your outhouse is full of human bones of people you have eaten."

It was pretty obvious to us that the people who came to our door weren't representatives of the doubters, but were, in fact, the doubters themselves. We opened the door of every closet and every building. One by one they looked down the toilet hole. They inspected the tins of food in our pantry. It was not easy to explain some of the labels. The canned mackerel had a picture of a fish on it. They had eaten corned beef from a tin picturing a cow. What would they eat from a tin of condensed milk with a picture of a smiling baby on it? However, the majority vote was in our favor. We would soon find out how significant the presence of those babies in our home would be.

The occasion was a terrible uprising of the Ekaris in the Wissel Lakes area. An epidemic of whooping cough was killing hundreds of little children. The leaders gathered to discuss the problem, squatting in a large circle on the ground and balancing their weight on their knees.

"Many of our children are dying. Why?"

"No doubt the spirits are very angry about something!"

"Why would the spirits be so angry?"

"Probably because of the foreigners in our land."

"What must we do?"

"Appease the spirits by eliminating the foreigners."

So a small army headed for our station. Naturally speaking, two unarmed young missionaries pitted against a task force of 50 well-armed warriors had little chance of survival.

As they passed through a nearby village, they explained, "As part of the patriotic effort to rid our land of the terrible coughing epidemic, we are going to eliminiate the devils in the metal-roofed house down there."

"Why are you telling us about it?" the villagers asked.

"Well, it seems like a big job for only 50 men. We're from out of town and wouldn't like to take on the job all by ourselves. How about joining forces with us and we'll do it together?"

"Those people are raising one of our babies for us," they responded, "and it wouldn't be right for us to help you. You'd best go elsewhere for allies."

Irritated but undaunted, they stomped out of the village and got back on the trail. At a second village, they again explained the purpose of their trip to Homeyo and invited the people in that village to join their ranks.

But the inhabitants of this village explained: "We took one of our babies to the people down in that metal-roofed house. They took it in and are caring for it. You'd best go elsewhere for help."

Within an hour's walk of our house there were many villages of people who would have been delighted with the opportunity to fill us with arrows, for there were always new rumors that we were indeed evil spirits.

For instance, a woman once entered the back door of the little bamboo house where we lived and sat on the floor beside our houseboy. They conversed quietly for a little while; then the woman began to weep, at first loudly, and then hysterically.

"Reddy," we asked the houseboy, "who is that woman and what is her problem?"

"That woman is my mother. She came to tell me that there is new evidence that you and Mama are really evil spirits and she is begging me to go home with her. She told me, 'They are deceiving you. They want to kill you. Come, my son, come home with me while there is still time for you to escape. Come! Come! I beg you, come with me now!' "

"But I told her, 'Mother, I know what I am talking about. They came here to tell us a beautiful story about the Chief of Heaven, how He loves people, and how He sent His Son to die for us. They are not evil spirits. They eat and sleep and work and play just like we do. They are good people. I won't go home with you. I am staying right here to help them so that they can do more work for the Chief of the Sky.' ''

We were indeed surrounded by enemy villages, but the sovereign God directed the warriors' steps to a third village from which we had also received a baby. Again the answer was no. These strong, brave warriors—earlier so confident and determined—returned to their valley, weeping because they could find no allies. Again, Satan's arrows were stopped by the shield which our Lord held in front of us and by the presence of some little native children.

''I am God, and there is no other;/ I am God, and there is none like me. I make known the end from the beginning,/ from ancient times, what is still to come./ I say: My purpose will stand,/ and I will do all that I please'' (Isaiah 46:9–10).

Billy, Dorothy, Leonard and Eva Cutts.

Bill and Gracie at Homeyo, 1950.

Bill, Gracie and Zani Mala enroute to Irian Jaya.

"Abraham and Sarah," Faith and Bill, Jr. in Goroka.

Rest stop on the trail. Ken Troutman (l.), Dr. L.L. King (r.), Gracie and Zani Mala.

Kiguabi.

Isa Sabo.

Gracie, Zani Mala and motherless children.

Alice-in-Wonderland, Faith and Bill, Jr.

Alice, Petrus and their children.

Gracie crossing swinging bridge.

Bill in the yard of the Hitadipa mission residence.

Pendeta Ototome, his wife and children.

Gracie and Yahya translating the scriptures.

John and his wife, Joy. John is the first second-generation Alliance missionary in Irian Jaya.

14

Zani Mala

G RACIE AND I BOTH LONGED to have children of our own, but it was time to go on our first furlough and there were none. We loved Alice Hope very much, but The Christian and Missionary Alliance policy is that missionaries can neither adopt nor marry the nationals of the land in which they are serving.

Having learned from the doctor that we would probably never have children of our own, we searched out an adoption agency in Binghamton, New York, where Rodimeer, Gracie's brother, and his wife had applied for a baby.

The agency received our application, but cautioned that there was not even a remote hope of completing the process in one year's time. But what was our Lord's will in the matter?

While we were studying at the Summer Institute of Linguistics, a letter from Gracie's mother announced exciting news. Rodimeer's turn had come up to receive a baby. What's more, Rod told the agency about his sister who also wanted to adopt a baby. He explained that she was a missionary who would have to leave the country in a few months. He asked them to permit her to take

71

"his" baby and to allow him to wait in line for the next one. "God will bless you for this, Rod," Gracie noted. And He did. Within a year, Rod's wife gave birth to a baby boy.

Course completed, we hurried back to Binghamton to meet our baby. He was a handsome, 18-month-old boy who was obviously delighted to meet us. We named him John Newton Cutts.

What excitement there was when this miniature white man entered the tribe! We were amazed at the way he opened doors that we had not been able to budge. Despite the persistent cries that we were evil spirits, strangers would often come into our yard and in no time Johnny would be sitting in their laps entertaining them. They reasoned that one couldn't get "zapped" too badly by such a miniature evil spirit!

Zani Mala was the Monis' name for him. They can't pronounce a J sound, so Johnny became Zani and Mala means *arrow*—one of their linguistic indicators that the name is masculine.

This little boy was the fulfillment of our prayers. Our arms wouldn't be empty and our hearts would be satisfied by children with whom we would share our lives.

"For the eyes of the Lord run to and fro throughout the whole earth, to shew himself strong in the behalf of them whose heart is perfect toward him" (2 Chronicles 16:9a KJV).

15

The Funeral Service

WE OPERATED A SCHOOL mainly for teaching the people to read to prepare them for the day when we would have the Scriptures translated into their language. The boys who attended needed food in order to continue in the school. We tried to buy potatoes for them, but frequently they were hungry because the people didn't bring enough on a regular basis. The thought came to mind: "Why not do as many others have done—plant a big garden and have the school self-supporting with the students tending the garden and eating the food it produces?" We decided to do it.

Keeping hungry, determined pigs out of a patch of sweet potatoes was more of a job than one would think. If a huge, hungry pig made up its mind that it was going to get the potatoes on the other side of the fence, it would do it by rooting under the fence, by gnashing the jungle-vine which tied the fence together or by backing off and ramming it. Besides, getting a fence built around the large area we envisioned—provided we could get someone to do it—would be quite costly. Another problem was that there was no

73

wood in the area that would last more than a couple of years exposed to the weather.

We used the rolls of barbed wire that we had brought back from furlough to put up a stock fence around our station. I hoped that it would discourage the most stout-hearted porker in the place and I thought that the people would be willing to walk around our fence. It didn't take long to see that the project was doomed to failure. We found the fence hiked up so far in places that a small-sized elephant could have gone under it without getting scratched.

One day while working on the fence, I came home feeling ill. "I think I will lie down for a little while," I told Gracie. As the day wore on, I felt worse and my temperature climbed to 104 degrees. The bed was soaked with perspiration.

The next morning when it was time for the Alliance radio "sched" (our name for the regular interstation calls), Gracie told Vida Troutman about my illness and the temperature that wouldn't go down. Dr. Ten Brink, the government's medical officer stationed at Enarotali, was called in on the case. He prescribed a full dose of quinine, which would take three days to complete. The three days dragged by with my temperature never dropping below 102.

At that time there were four other missionaries on our station at Homeyo: Gordon and Peggy Larson, and two single women, Leona St. John and Rosalie Fenton. Rosalie was a registered nurse, but she and her partner had left the station a week before to vacation on the coast. The trip to the coast was the same as it had been when we came to New Guinea: a three-day hike over the trail and then flying boat from Enarotali.

Vida reported to Dr. Ten Brink that the quinine course had been completed, but my condition had not changed. The doctor said, "I think I know what Mr. Cutts has. The symptoms are those of scrub typhus, which is caused by the bite of a wood tick. More soldiers fighting in New Guinea died of that disease than those who died from bullets. Unfortunately I have nothing in my drug supply that can help him."

Vida replied, "We have a nurse stationed at Homeyo who just went through here on her way to the coast. There were some packages here for her, including drug samples."

Vida showed the packages to Dr. Ten Brink. It was Terramycin—the very thing that could help me.

The next broadcast from Vida was indeed an encouraging one: "Tell Bill not to give up. We found some medicine that will help him, and Ken has a couple of carriers on the way with it. He told them that it was urgent to get it there as soon as possible and they promised to run. They should be there the day after tomorrow."

Day number six dawned. I was growing weaker and weaker. Gracie kept up the spongings to bring down the fever, but it seemed that my brain was burning out. The day wore on. It was getting dark and I knew they could not travel over the rough trail at night.

Day number seven. Surely having spent the night nearby, they would be here shortly after sunup! But again the sun reached its zenith and again began its descent.

We had been contacting Enarotali frequently by radio. Vida couldn't imagine why the carriers hadn't arrived. Then day number eight dawned and it was again time for the morning "sched." Vida's voice betrayed her anxiety. "The carriers got back here last evening. They tried and tried to get to you, but the rivers were at flood stage and they couldn't get through. We have contacted Mission Aviation Fellowship at Sentani and Dave Steiger said that he would come here tomorrow morning, get the medicine and make a drop to you. Keep hanging on. We're all praying."

Early morning of day number nine. I was getting weaker and losing weight rapidly. At such a rate I knew I would be in heaven by this time tomorrow! I had purchased some hand-split boards to make something; they were visible from the bedroom window. I thought, *I suppose they will use those boards to make me a coffin.* It was a blessed thought. No panic or fear. *Tomorrow I'll be with my Lord who loved me and gave Himself for me!* I was concerned about Gracie and four-year-old Zani Mala, but my mind was too weak to worry about it for long.

Soon we heard the drone of a small aircraft in the distance. Dave came low over our station, buzzed the plateau a few hundred feet above our house, and dropped the precious packet in a bog of 12-foot reeds.

Having been the "official nurse" on the station before Rosalie's arrival, I opened the package, read the instruction sheet and took the prescribed dosage.

A lot of time had elapsed. It was late afternoon when Gordon, Peggy and a group of nationals came up to my bedroom. Perhaps they sang a song, I don't remember, but I clearly remember Gordon reading the Twenty-third Psalm. My national friends were weeping audibly. They were sure that it was the farewell to their "father." I would say that before a person dies is the perfect time for the funeral so that he or she can enjoy seeing all his or her friends and know how much they care.

While everyone was carrying on, there was a knock at the door. Who could it be? Not a national, for they never knock—they stand in front of a door and yell. Gracie went downstairs and opened the door. It was Dr. Ten Brink! Impossible! There was no way that a European could cover all that ground in only twelve hours of daylight. But it was really him! He had left Enarotali in the predawn hours, coming up the river by flashlight. The very high water that had prevented the carriers getting through had enabled him to run his boat further up the river than ever before. They had jumped out of the boat and run the rest of the way, arriving just minutes before sunset.

He told Gracie to clear the room and let in some fresh air. He checked on the amount of Terramycin that I had taken and gave me an injection of something he had brought with him, perhaps penicillin. Then he searched my body carefully trying to locate the miniature cone-shaped hole that would verify his diagnosis. There it was, the mark of the tick that produces scrub typhus.

My Lord was perfectly capable of healing me apart from any medication as He had several times in the past. But the way He did heal me— orchestrating to the minute many of the details involved—certainly brought praise to Him.

In all of earth and all of heaven, is there any being like the Lord our God?

16

Runway 1

I N THE FALL OF 1955, word came over the two-way
radio that our friend Dick Lenehan was coming to visit us in Homeyo. Enroute to New
Guinea for our second term, Dick, his wife Edna
and their three young children had been fellow-
passengers on a Dutch freighter, the MS *Bali*.
Dick had come to the field to do maintenance
work on the new Short Sealand amphibian. The
first plane had crashed into the side of a mountain on April 28, 1955, killing its pilot, Al Lewis.

Dick arrived at the station with an interesting
announcement. The Alliance officials had decided that the work of supplying missionaries in
interior New Guinea could be done more effec-
tively and efficiently if smaller aircraft, capable of
landing at any station, would be purchased.
Headquarters was in the process of purchasing a
couple of "Sessners"—Dick's Boston pronuncia-
tion of Cessna—to start with. Gracie wrote her
mother with the exciting news that our trail trips
to Enarotali were about to end. Her mother wrote
back saying, "Grace Betty, I have looked in a
number of flying magazines and asked a lot of

people, but I haven't been able to find out what a Sessner is!''

Dick assured me that we could find a place for the plane to land at our station and the search for an air strip site began. About a five-minute walk to the east and a hundred feet above our house was a plateau that had been formed by a landslide many years before. It ran at a right angle to the valley. The base of a mountain formed one end of the plateau which then extended 1200 feet to the other end. Regardless of the weight of any load, if a plane were to take off starting from the base of the mountain, it was certain to be airborne when it reached the 1200-foot mark because that point was the edge of a cliff! At its base, nearly a thousand feet below, the Kemabu River snaked through the Kemandoga Valley.

"Ah, just the place," Dick assured us. "The 'Sessner' can land in a thousand feet if it has to." The altitude of the plateau was about 5,000 feet so any pilot reading this will be glad that he didn't fly for the Alliance in those days. The Mission Aviation Fellowship pilots who later would land at Homeyo referred to it as the "suicide strip."

My courses at Nyack did not include airstrip construction, but that didn't matter—all of my equally ignorant missionary colleagues were building airstrips at their stations, too.

The job was herculean. At the precipice end there was a giant mound of clay approximately eight feet high. Several hundred feet up the strip site was a huge depression—at its lowest point about eight feet lower than the surrounding area.

No problem here—just slide the hump into the hollow. Nothing to it—for a bulldozer! But men chipping little chunks of clay off the mound with ordinary garden forks and other men and boys, women and girls carrying the chunks on their heads or on litters made of gunnysack to the depression a few hundred feet distant was a different story. It seemed that the depression would never be filled. The level of the clay in the huge hole always appeared exactly the same as it was yesterday, or the day before yesterday, or the day before that. The day came, however, when we had about 800 feet of level, hard runway.

There was a totally different construction problem for the remaining 400 feet. This area was covered with a thick jungle of reeds about 12 feet tall. When we finished cutting these and carried them off, a fairly level surface of soft black muck was revealed. At different points I pushed a long reed down into it. As I "climbed" the reed, it sank into the soft ground—all 12 feet of it.

We noticed that surface water was running down the mountain onto the strip site, so we dug a deep, wide ditch across the site at the base of the mountain. If a plane couldn't get stopped at the end of the runway, the ditch would be an effective device for halting it so that it wouldn't start climbing the mountain! The water from this ran into another ditch which was dug down one side of the site to the edge of the precipice.

The ground didn't get dry and hard as we had hoped. Someone noticed that water from an unknown source was running into the second ditch. A closer look revealed a lovely spring right in the middle of the future runway! I asked the other missionaries on the station to save me all their empty tin cans. I dug little ditches from the spring area to the main ditch and laid my "ground pipe"—tin cans opened at both ends, wired together and covered with dirt. In time the surface began to dry out.

Our biggest problem was the lack of labor. Available hands were becoming fewer and fewer. We were giving a steel axe head for two weeks of work. Everyone wanted to work the first two weeks and we had a long waiting list because I didn't want the number of workers to outnumber my supply of tools. We gave out the axes at the end of the first two-week period and the next crew took over. After the next two-week period the same thing happened. But the time came, with mountains of work still to be done, that there was no waiting list. We asked some, "Why don't you work another two weeks and get another axe?"

"It requires two hands to operate an axe," they responded, "and I have only two hands. What would I do with two axes?"

A few of them were persuaded to sign up; a few even earned three axes. Scouts were sent far and wide to enlist the workers we needed to finish the job. One group was from the village of Mogalo, an hour or so distant from our station. The people of that village had not yet received the gospel, but the chief and many of his men signed up to work. It's difficult to find exactly the right word for those men. In other areas of New Guinea there were real chiefs; some had the power of life and death over their subjects. But it was different in Moni land: everyone was a chief!

I went to lunch one day while the Mogalo group was working and returned to find that they had built a lean-to, covered it with reeds to shelter themselves from the rays of the noonday sun, and were all having a siesta. The contract I had made with all who worked was an axe head for 12 eight-hour days. I explained to the villagers that the axes were not mine, but that they were given to me by the children of the Chief of the Sky, so they belonged to Him. By loafing as they were, they were not stealing from me, but were robbing the Chief of Heaven. Actually, in my "righteous" indignation I may have told them that they were common horse thieves, totally devoid of any remote semblance of integrity or moral standards and had no doubt come from a long line of ancestors of the same calibre!

The Mogalo chief sprang to his feet, put an arrow on his bowstring and pulled it back as far as it would go. All of his followers immediately jumped aside to form a wide arena in which he could operate without fear of shooting the wrong person. There he stood facing me, only a few feet away, his arrow pointed at my chest. Even a drunk couldn't miss at that range, and Monis didn't drink in those days. I began to think that perhaps I had completed the task to which my Lord called me and I wondered, once more, how Gracie and Zani Mala would get on without me.

"You're unarmed," the chief said. "Shooting you would be like shooting a woman. Go home and get your bow and arrows. Then return and we'll have a duel."

At that point I thought I was about to preach my last sermon, so I wanted it to be a good one. "I didn't come all the way from my country to fight duels. I came to tell you about the Chief of Heaven who loves you very much—so much that He sent His Son to this earth to die for you." As I preached on, the point of the arrow lowered a little and the tension on the bowstring relaxed. Finally, the arrow tip was pointing at the ground. The chief took the arrow off the string, laid his weapons on the ground, and with his men went back to work.

There was a large deposit of a strange kind of clay that "just happened" to be alongside the strip. I dug off a piece and laid it on the strip. The next day I noticed that the piece was very hard. I called some tribesmen over. "This is interesting stuff. It was soft yesterday and now it is very hard. What will happen to it if the rain hits it?"

"It will stay hard, Tuani."

There's my answer, I thought. *I will build a big "snowshoe" for this bog out of that clay.* By that time, we were down to half a dozen men and two wheelbarrows. I said to the men, "All you have to do is keep these wheelbarrows full all day long. I will wheel a load of clay from the pit to the strip, dump it and return for the next barrow. I want it to be full when I get back." So it went, hour after hour, day after day.

I had been working on the strip for nearly a year, first as engineer, going up to the site, giving instructions for the day, and returning home to do translation work. Then I became supervisor, staying with the people exacting as much work as possible from the diminishing force. Finally, I joined the work crew. I was continually exhausted and came home in the late afternoon almost too tired to eat.

The mission was urging me over the two-way radio to get the job done. "Bill, we need the strip for this lifetime, you know." No other strip had taken as long to build as ours. Finally I said, "I have 800 feet of good, hard, dry clay surface. After that there are 200 feet of dry bog land with a layer of clay 'snowshoe.' The last 200 feet is bog land without a clay covering. If the pilot can get his wheels solidly on the ground the instant he is over the strip, and if he can brake hard on the clay surface, maybe he can stop before he gets to the end of my 'snowshoe' at the 1,000-foot mark."

"Okay, Bill. Ed Ulrich will be in to your station the day after tomorrow. We will be praying for good weather."

The great day arrived. Hundreds of Monis lined the airstrip on both sides eager to see the landing of the noisy bird that had circled around just over their heads so many times. Down valley we heard the drone of the engine. The Cessna 180 went out to the far edge of the valley, then aligned itself with the runway. Closer and closer it came. Then it was over the end of the runway. "Get her down, Ed; get her DOWN," every part of me was screaming. A precious hundred feet of runway rolled back of the plane untouched. Then another hundred and another. The wheels finally made solid contact with the ground. The tail wheel was way up in the air, indicating that Ed was breaking as hard as he dared.

The rest of the 800 feet rolled behind the plane. He was on the snowshoe. My snowshoe was doing as I had hoped, holding up the plane as it continued to brake. One hundred feet went by and then the second hundred. The plane was almost stopped. The front wheels dropped off the snowshoe and sank into the bog, bringing the plane to an abrupt halt. The tail slowly raised. Surely the tail wheel would drop back down when the plane stopped! But it didn't. Up, up, ever so slowly it went like a movie on slow speed. The tall, vertical tail-fin sliced into the bog. The plane lay like a slain bird with its belly toward the sun and its spindly legs grotesquely clutching the air.

Suddenly, all the tensions of the preceding months burst from my being in audible sobs. One of my national friends, Tao Tagapa Bega, asked, "What is the matter with you? Is there anything unusual about the way it landed?"

Ed's passenger that day was the government's

Director of Civil Aviation, Mr. W.P. Hamers. He suggested a list of things that were needed to rectify the plane—a couple of long poles, some shorter poles, rope, a pulley if I had one, and some jungle vine. Very soon, Juliet-Zulu-Papa-Tango-Charlie again stood on its spindly legs, a bit shame-faced perhaps and in need of a bath, but otherwise virtually unharmed.

17

The Macedonians

IT WAS THE SPRING OF 1959. Three years earlier, in order to open the Ilaga Valley to the gospel, Gordon Larson and Don Gibbons had made an overland trek.

Before Gordon went to the Danis of the Ilaga to do language reduction work and translate the Scriptures into their language, he and Peggy had been stationed with us at Homeyo. We had worked together on deciphering the Moni language. After they left, I continued the job of reducing it to writing and then produced a short textbook to help new missionaries to learn the language.

Gracie and I had developed a series of primers to teach the people to read and a set of readers to go with them. I had translated the Gospel of John and other books of the New Testament. Meanwhile, we had completed the airstrip and built a large two-story house.

A single man, Harold Catto, had joined our forces at Homeyo, and together we had done the building. Gracie, ever working for Cupid, thought that it would be nice for Harold to get better acquainted with Mary McIlrath, a lovely young woman who had been one of our hostesses when we arrived as new missionaries. Harold had met Mary at Enarotali while he was preparing for the trail trip to Homeyo. Now Gracie arranged for Harold to do some mission business in Enarotali. It didn't take long for Cupid's arrow to strike— permanently!

It was at this point that some strangers came to our door saying, "We are from the Dugindoga Valley. We have heard a little of the story about the Chief of the Sky and about His Son. We and our people back home are very hungry to hear more. There are six of you missionaries living here in the Homeyo area and the people have heard the good news for many years. We ask that two of you leave Homeyo and come to the Dugindoga to live with us and tell us more about the Chief of the Sky."

How had the peoples of the Dugindoga Valley heard the story of the Chief of the Sky? It began with the tribes of the Ilaga Valley—the Danis and the Damals. When the Damals received the gospel, they immediately thought of their unbelieving friends and relatives in the Beoga, a small valley several walking days to the west. So it was that brand-new national Christians hurried to the Beoga with the good news.

This marvellous awakening was reminiscent of the game of dominoes, the first pushing over the second, the second the third, and so on until the whole lineup is affected. The Holy Spirit, firing the hearts and anointing the lips of the newly born-again nationals, was multiplying the message with power. The people of the Beoga received the gospel and they thought of their friends and clan members living several days to the west in the Dugindoga Valley. The Dugindoga was unique in that old tribal wars had caused people of several tribes to inhabit that valley. It was Moni for the most part, but there were also Danis and Damals living there with some members of still smaller tribes. And so the Beoga Damals came to the Dugindoga with their exciting news.

But there was another factor in this amazing story. A young married Moni man from the Dugindoga by the name of Ototome was visiting in the Beoga about the time the gospel arrived there from the Ilaga. Upon hearing the good news from their Damal neighbors and also from Ototome, the Dugindoga Monis sent the delegation to Homeyo to beg for missionaries to come and live among them.

Gracie and I were getting ready to go on furlough when the "Macedonians" arrived at our door. We told them more about the Chief of Heaven and we prayed with them. We told them to keep praying and that our Lord would certainly undertake for them. But their concerns were pretty much dismissed from our minds as furlough was coming up and we were concentrating on making arrangements to adopt a baby sister for Zani Mala.

One year later we returned to the field with

baby Amy Grace, just in time to attend the field conference. There we learned that the "Macedonians" weren't about to give up on their request. They had made more trips to Homeyo while we were in the United States. The big question before conference was: "Whom will we send to the Dugindoga?"

I reasoned that if I returned to Homeyo after the conference, I could just open up our cabinets and be back in the translation business in a few days. It was to that work that the sovereign God had called the "weak thing." If we were to volunteer to open the Dugindoga, who knew how many years it would be before we could begin translating again? Temporary living quarters would have to be built. Another airstrip would have to be constructed—I was still groaning at the remembrance of the last one! A permanent mission residence would have to be built. Could it be that my Lord would want me to put the translation of His Word on a back burner and build a new station first?

Rosalie and Leona, the two single women living on our station at that time, were willing to go, but it was thought that the job was no undertaking for two single women. No one else offered to go, so that narrowed the "volunteer" supply down to Gracie and me. We earnestly prayed that our Lord would plainly reveal His will in the matter.

The inner voice said, "I want you to go there."

We were about to find out what fantastic blessings accompany the believer's immediate obedience to the voice of the Lord!

18

Serendipity

THE WORD *SERENDIPITY* HINTS at how Gracie and I discovered sheer joy and blessing as we obeyed the Lord, pulling up roots in Homeyo and moving into the Dugindoga.

Harold Catto, who by that time had become field chairman, and I flew from Homeyo to Pogapa where we spent the night. Early next morning we started on the nearly two-day trek to Hitadipa, the principal settlement in the Dugindoga Valley.

Gracie and I had spent nearly 10 years in cold, hard, unresponsive Homeyo. What Harold and I saw and heard as we moved into the new area was hard to believe. We were stopped time and time again by large gatherings of people shouting: *"Hazi ndona! Hazi ndona!"*—"We are hungry for *hazi.*" When Sunday morning came, we could hear large groups of people chanting in unison on their way to the open-air service. We estimated that about 1500 people gathered for the meeting, eagerly awaiting the *hazi* talk from their very own missionary.

It was July 1960. Gracie was still at Homeyo waiting for the mission boarding school on the coast at Sentani to open so that Zani Mala would not have to walk into the Dugindoga and then walk back out again when school opened. In mid August he climbed into the little Cessna airplane that had braved the "suicide" strip at Homeyo. The following day, Gracie flew to Pogapa to set out on the trail with one-year-old Amy Grace. Gracie was the first European woman ever to travel alone on the interior highland trails.

Carriers, who had joyously gone over the trail to Pogapa to meet their new "Mama" and baby, accompanied her. Unaware that Gracie could not maintain their pace on the trail, they set out at full speed to the village where they expected to spend the night. With them was Gracie's sleeping bag, food, blankets for the baby and other things that make a night on the trail more endurable. The convoy had dwindled down to Gracie and the lone native carrying Amy—soon to be named Hitadipa Sama—in his net. Just before sunset they reached a little village where there was a hut where Gracie could sleep. The local people gave her some of their food and the carrier loaned her his blanket so that baby Amy would be comfortable during the chilly night.

No welcome for Queen Elizabeth could have been more sincere or more festive than that given by the people of the Dugindoga for Gracie and Amy when they arrived at Hitadipa. Pigs by the score were butchered and put into the pits where New Guinea's interior tribespeople cook their festive food. The normal weather pattern for the highlands is rain from late afternoon until the wee hours of the morning. But after Gracie arrived, there were some lovely moonlit nights when we would sit on logs with the people on the new airstrip site. Huge burning piles of tree branches made a cozy setting. One night the moon was very red and we told them about the coming of our Lord when the moon would be "turned to blood."

They really meant it when they cried, "*Hazi ndona.*" They couldn't hear enough about the Chief of Heaven, the amazing things that His Son did, and His wonderful Word. For weeks they came to where we slept at night and yelled until we woke up. They did not come because someone was gravely ill and needed help, but because they had forgotten how a certain Bible verse went and needed their memories refreshed.

How could only two missionaries evangelize and teach such a large group of people? And because of the different tribes coexisting there, our teaching would have to be done in at least three languages. We surely needed God's wisdom and direction as we faced the tremendous job that our new flock presented.

"There are very many of you," we told the people, "and you live scattered in so many directions. It is impossible for two missionaries to teach you all about the Chief of Heaven and His Son unless you help us."

"Sure we will help you. What do you want us to do?"

"We want you to bring poles and jungle vine and tree bark. We are going to build a little school here. We want two men chosen from each village to attend our school."

Thus the Hitadipa witness school began. About 50 men ranging from teenage to middle age, including Monis, Danis, Ndugas, Damals and a few Dems, enthusiastically began attending. They were totally illiterate, but they were exactly who God needed to open the Dugindoga to the gospel. While I worked on building the airstrip, Gracie taught the men. School began each Tuesday morning. For four days she worked on getting a short Bible passage and its application into their minds. It was necessary for her to drill them over and over again. When a few people "got it" they would go outdoors with a small group to continue drilling on their own.

Friday at noon, the students would fan out in every possible direction to preach the things they had learned. Similar to the workings of God that are recorded in the book of the Acts, God witnessed with signs and wonders to the truth of what the students preached. Some of the villages were far away and it would take the students until Saturday to arrive. The students would give the entire weekend to preaching, and return to Hitadipa on Monday to be ready for the next week of memorization.

Those Tuesday school openings were precious as the students gave glowing reports of what God had done as they preached and prayed. Scores of people were healed. Demons were cast out. They told of going to one hut where they asked the owner if they could have a gospel service in his home. He replied, "Fine, go ahead. You may preach all you like. You may sing all you like, but don't pray!"

As the service continued, the students noticed that the landlord had gone to sleep. Happily they exclaimed, "Now is our opportunity to pray," and proceeded to do just that. Instantly, the landlord was up like a maniac waving his arms, screaming and shouting. In Jesus' name the students commanded the demon to leave the man. It obeyed, and the man, together with the rest of his villagers, sat down again to listen to the new *hazi* talk.

The students even reported that God raised some people from the dead in answer to their prayers. Hundreds of people near and far were convinced of the truth of the gospel and wanted "to take the mind of Jesus" and be baptized. We wanted to ensure that they knew what the Christian life was all about before they participated in that ordinance, so we recorded the catechism on a couple of tapes and blared them from battery-operated tape recorders on two corners of our front lawn. They would really get the gospel message "into their stomachs."

In 1961, since there were no ordained nationals, it fell to me to do all the baptizing. The altitude at Hitadipa was about 5,000 feet, but the water flowed from elevations much higher; it was freezing cold. After immersing people hour after hour, my body was shaking and my teeth were chattering. I was sure that I would never be warm again.

The new airstrip was really beautiful. It was built on an old river bed and the slope was even for all of its 2,100 feet. Building an airstrip this time was comparatively easy. When we left Homeyo, Isa Sabo—the man who helped me with Bible translation—had said, "Where you go, I will go." So it was that our two families moved together. I laid out the strip, sighted from one end to the other with binoculars and put notches in poles sunk along the sides of the strip at 25-foot intervals. I taught Isa Sabo to put a string across the strip from one notch to the other. Any land that was higher than the string would have to be sliced off; any below the string would have to be filled in. That freed me to do other work while my foreman and hundreds of workers built the strip.

It was impossible to pay for labor. The locals wanted the gospel to come to their area. They had called us to come to teach them and they were going to build the airstrip! When it was finished, all they permitted us to do to show our gratitude for their work was to fly in a few sacks of salt. These they divided among themselves.

There isn't space here for me to elaborate about God's continuing work in Hitadipa—the witness school which turned into a Bible school with national teachers; the many pastors and wives who shepherded about 35 churches scattered around the Dugindoga; the more than 2,000 baptized ers.

is the One who called the "weak thing" into His service. He is the One who said, "I am with you all the days." He is the One who overruled in my countless blunders.

"This poor man called, and the Lord heard him;/ he saved him out of all his troubles./ The angel of the Lord encamps around those who fear him,/ and he delivers them./ Taste and see that the Lord is good;/ blessed is the man who takes refuge in him./ Fear the Lord, you his saints,/ for those who fear him lack nothing./ The lions may grow weak and hungry, but those who seek the Lord lack no good thing" (Psalm 34:6–10).

19

Runaway River

WAY BACK ON LABOR DAY 1942, the day I fully dedicated my life to the Lord, Mrs. Stull had made an interesting observation—that in this life we can see only the confusing back side of the tapestry on which the Master Weaver is working. I recalled her statement as we neared the completion of the airstrip.

Our beautiful 2,100-foot-long airstrip was being threatened by the river that flowed beside it. We had chosen a level site covered with trees two feet or more in diameter. Although we considered its proximity to the river, we assumed that the water had not been near the area for years. However, soon after the strip was completed we saw that it had not been a wise decision. We tried to straighten the channel upriver to keep it from eroding the bank by the strip. We even built a jetty to deflect the flow.

The jetty was built from a cage of heavy woven wire fencing about 10 feet wide and extended far out into the river at a 45-degree angle with the shoreline. We filled the cage with rocks—tons and tons of them. But during each heavy downpour, the river became very powerful, carrying logs and huge boulders in its current. As the boulders hit the wire fencing of the jetty, it would break, letting the rocks spill out. We ordered two plane loads of steel airstrip webbing that had been discarded by the government when the new asphalt strip was built at Sentani. It took several weeks to wire the plates to the upper side of the cage, but finally the jetty was bringing an end to the erosion of the bank.

All of us worked hours and hours attempting to avert the impending calamity. The interior nationals can carry very heavy loads on their backs for hours on end, but curiously enough, it seemed almost impossible for them to pick up a heavy boulder out of the river bed and place it on their shoulders. So Gracie became the "crane" who elevated the boulder onto the shoulders of the waiting carriers. Then, when their color changed from brown to blue from working in the frigid water, she would run home and make a bucket of hot coffee for them.

Another complication was that two rivers, the Hiabu and the Dogabu, converged a few hundred feet above the upper end of the strip. The flow by the strip depended on which of the two tributaries was the stronger at the moment.

One day some nationals came running to our door to tell us that there was no water in the Hiabu and that we'd better go to higher ground. If a large dam formed and let go all at once, it could be dangerous downstream. We grabbed baby Amy and our important papers and went to a native hut on higher ground. It turned out to be a false alarm.

But the respite was short-lived. One weekend Gracie went to a village a few hours distant for ministry. I stayed with Amy. That night there was an unusually heavy downpour of rain that continued hour after hour. The river rose until it was a few inches below the doorway of our house. I had already positioned my briefcase for a quick exit but about midnight the downpour stopped. A while later I could see that the water had receded. When it became obvious that all was safe, I went to bed. I was never able to sleep well again until we moved into the new house on the hill where the river would never reach us.

A check of the runway the next morning revealed that about 1,100 feet had been washed downstream. I announced on the two-way radio that this would be a good day for the Lord to come! The nationals sat on the river bank and looked at the fast-moving stream that had been our airstrip. They were weeping and putting into words what was in my mind also: "Why has this happened? Is it because the Chief of the Sky doesn't love us and is keeping us from hearing any more about the gospel? Our missionaries won't be able to stay here without an airstrip and we will be the same as we were before they came to us with the *hazi* talk."

The enemy had hurled a powerful spear, but God knew about it all the time. By then, the Mission Aviation Fellowship was flying for all missions working in New Guinea. The head pilot of MAF in Irian Jaya was Hank Worthington, a man who feared only God. Hank came on the radio, "How much of the strip do you have left, Bill?"

"One thousand feet."

"Okay, tack 200 feet onto that and I'll come in."

What rejoicing and thanksgiving there was as Hank dropped his wheels on the "tacked on" section and braked to a stop before he ran out of runway. But Hank was more adventuresome than most pilots and we immediately explored the valley floor for another site. With Hank's concurrence, we settled on one as far away from the river as possible. The new strip would be a few hundred feet shorter than the one it replaced with a dog-leg about 300 feet from the upper end. The people worked enthusiastically and the work progressed smoothly and quickly.

All the while, the new strip was being built, the 200-foot section added onto the old runway was something like a roll-away bed one uses for guests. When Hank notified us of his arrival day, a group of nationals would carry rock and gravel to the washed out place and smooth it and Hank would come in with a load of supplies. Then if we had more than a very light rainfall in the afternoon, the river would wash out the new section again. Needless to say, we were glad when the new strip was completed.

Opening the new station at Hitadipa in the Dugindoga Valley had been time-consuming. While Gracie was teaching the witness school students, foreman Isa Sabo was directing the work force at the strip and I was building a temporary house that we could live in. The house was 12 feet wide and 22 feet in length and had two stories. When Hitadipa opened in 1960, Gordon Larson and Don Gibbons had put together a 10-by-10-foot shed. That shed became our dining room, pantry and baby Amy's bedroom. Gracie did our cooking on a tiny wood stove located just outside the door of the shed. Our own bedroom was a nine-by-nine-foot tent.

As Gracie became more and more disenchanted with the joys of camping, I promised her that on a certain night we would be sleeping in our new house.

When the frame was completed, I laid the floors and finished the walls with split boards we had purchased from the people. But on the morning of the move-in day there was still no roof. From my youth I had done my best to live in such a way that my word was as good as my bond. Now I had a problem. There was no way that I could put up the ridge pole, get the rafters and sheathing in place and put on the aluminum sheets all in one day. Even so, we slept in our new house as I had promised. I pitched our tent on the second-story floor!

20

Cutts Money

IT WAS SHORTLY AFTER the takeover of Irian Jaya by the Indonesian government that—only because of our Lord's intervention—we were not thrown out of the country for printing money!

Store items such as clothing were hard to come by in the interior highlands where we lived. A lot of the interior people had Indonesian rupiah notes, but they couldn't use them to buy very much unless they took a trip to the coast.

The interior missionaries needed to have nationals do work for them—maintaining the airstrips and mission buildings and working in the missionaries' homes—to free them for the Lord's work. At that time, the barter system was seldom used and we paid cash for labor, food, firewood and other things. This meant we had to import all sorts of merchandise from the coast. We would send out order forms; the purchasing agents of the various missions would purchase the items; and then Mission Aviation Fellowship planes would bring in the freight. It irked us to have to neglect our primary duties to become merchants, but there seemed to be no other way to get people to work for us or to bring us produce.

I felt I had a workable solution to the problem. We had a spirit-duplicator and several bottles of ink of different colors. I made master copies of promissory notes of various denominations. For example: "I promise to pay the bearer of this piece of paper five rupiahs." I signed my name at the bottom of the note.

People came to us to purchase things they wanted and we explained that we didn't have the time or strength to operate a store for the whole population of the interior. "If you need something from the stores on the coast," we told them, "you can bring vegetables or firewood or work on the strip and we will pay you in 'Cutts money,' which you can then spend in our store."

At that time the Indonesian government organized a joint Indonesian-Japanese expedition to climb to Sukarno Top, one of the snow-covered mountain peaks southeast of Hitadipa. The members of the expedition flew to the Wissel Lakes, obtained porters, and walked to our station. They spent a number of days there getting ready for the climb. As they entered our area they were low on food and attempted to purchase some in the villages they passed through, offering Indonesian rupiahs in payment. The villagers said, "This money is no good. If you pay us in Cutts money, we will sell you our food."

One of the men in the group—a petty officer— was a well-educated Irianese who had a different religious persuasion than ours. He immediately saw a splendid opportunity to get us expelled from the country. He exchanged some of his belongings for several of our promissory notes. He intended to take them to the officials on the coast as evidence that we were engaged in subversive activities. Had his plan succeeded, not only would Gracie and I have been expelled from the country, but there would have been a lot of embarrassment for our mission.

The day after the expedition arrived in Hitadipa was the birthday of its leader, Lt. Col. H.A. Hamid. Gracie made a birthday cake for him and we invited him and his subordinates to a party at our house. We had excellent rapport with the personnel of the expedition while they were on our station. A day or so after the party, Lt. Col. Hamid brought up the subject of the Cutts money. I explained my impression that one could give out promissory notes anywhere in the world. "Well, that would certainly be true in Surabaya or Jakarta," Hamid replied, "but here, where we are trying to acquaint the people with our ways of doing things, it would be best to use only our rupiahs as currency. However, to set your mind at ease, I ordered my petty officer to give me all the promissory notes he collected and I have destroyed them."

After the expedition successfully climbed the peak, the government published a book about it. Gracie and I were cited for helping the expedition in various ways and there was a half-page photo of Gracie and me with Amy and another photo of Amy riding on the shoulders of a national.

And, thank the Lord, there was no mention of Cutts money. I am reminded of Romans 8:31b: ''If God is for us, who can be against us?''

21

The Birthday Present

W E HAD BEEN WORKING AMONG THE MONIS for 14 years and our assignment by the mission, which we had accepted as an assignment by the sovereign God, had been to translate the Bible into a tribal language. Now, 14 years later, in the spring of 1964, it appeared that I could finally begin the job I had been sent to do. The building of three airstrips, two houses and a number of other buildings—including a two-story bookstore and classrooms for the Bible school— was behind me. Gracie and I had been the sole teachers at the witness/Bible school. We had also been training nationals to take more and more of the workload. Down the line as far as I could see the tracks looked clear.

Gracie wanted to take a course, which was being offered at Enarotali, on new changes in the Indonesian language, so she and five-year-old Amy boarded the plane. As Gracie's birthday is June 20 and Amy's is June 24, I decided to surprise them with a birthday gift upon their return.

Because there had been quite a bit of illness— diarrhea and hepatitis—among missionaries, our field leaders legislated that the outhouse of each mission residence should be eliminated and replaced by its counterpart within the house. The plumbing fixtures and ground pipe had been stored in our shed, waiting until I had time to tackle the project.

I started with the septic tank, cutting the bottom out of a 50-gallon drum and wiring it to another drum in order to make a cylinder about six feet high and two feet in diameter.

When it came time to connect the flush tank to the toilet bowl I discovered that I could not join the two pieces of iron pipe because the outside diameter of the one was exactly the same as the inside diameter of the other. I decided to get out my hand-turned grinding wheel to modify one of the pipes.

Gracie and Amy returned to Hitadipa to find their birthday present completed. I wrapped white paper around the tank, added a big red ribbon and wrote: "Happy Birthday, Mama and Amy."

At some point during the construction of the bath my right eye began to hurt, irritated perhaps because of a stray chip from the grinding wheel. I could endure the pain as I worked during the day, but I was unable to sleep at night. Since I was the station nurse, I had quite an assortment of drugs that I had received from the mission doctors. Among them was a bottle of cocaine drops. At bedtime I would put two drops into my eye, sleep for a while, wake up in pain and put in two more. This was the same eye that at birth had been dangling on my cheek by its cords. It did have some vision if I held a book in just the right position and at the right distance.

During our first term on the field I had picked up an eye disease in this same eye. A yellow film had formed in one corner and spread over the eye. This was followed by a blackish colored film. We had nothing with which to fight the disorder so I had headed for Enarotali. By the time I arrived, I was also experiencing a lot of discomfort in my good eye. Mary McIlrath had some excellent ophthalmic ointment and treated me until my good eye cleared up. The right eye, however, had become blind.

Now with this new eye problem as a result of the grinding wheel chip, the field doctors were becoming very concerned. They thought that perhaps a complete rest might strengthen my body sufficiently for it to fight the iritis that was raging in my good eye. We decided to go to Nabire on the north coast of New Guinea. I was confined to bed in a darkened room except for meals and an hour at the beach in the late afternoon after the sun's glare had diminished. But the eye continued to deteriorate.

It was then decided that I should go to an ophthalmologist in Port Moresby. After examining me, the doctor said that it would be best for him to replace the eye with a prosthesis, a procedure called enucleation. But there was one problem— he had only brown eyes in his collection and no blue ones! Instead, he gave me a bottle of cortisone eye drops and some tablets.

The result was astounding! The doctor and I both rejoiced at the apparent miracle that had taken place. As we parted, he gave me instructions to taper off the cortisone in a couple of days.

While I was still using small amounts of cortisone, the trouble reappeared. Later doctors would tell me that cortisone is known as "the deceptive drug." It is like putting a blanket over a fire to contain it. While the blanket is in place, all that remains is a couple of thin wisps of smoke. But when the blanket is removed, the fire bursts into flames.

Sympathetic ophthalmia was destroying my good eye. Satan had once more struck a master blow. It appeared that the "weak thing" whom the sovereign God had called to give His Word to lost tribespeople would never return to New Guinea soil.

But the eternal, almighty, all-knowing God was—as always—unsurprised and ready with His counter-thrust! Our mission doctors concurred that I was in serious trouble and should return to the States immediately on an early medical furlough. Regular furlough was still a number of months away. Now there were all sorts of urgent preparations for leaving. For example, one of the field auditors, according to procedure, had to come and examine the station books. Thank God for missionary Mary Owen! When she observed

me trying to balance the books with drawn
shades because of the painful sensitivity to light,
she offered to finish the job for me.

The pain in my good eye grew more intense as
the sympathetic ophthalmia accelerated. The trip
home would not include the usual good time
visiting "faraway places with strange-sounding
names." Headquarters had selected an ophthalmologist in New York City, Dr. Payne, who was
getting ready to retire.

Eventually I found myself in a chair in Dr.
Payne's office as he examined my eyes with a slit
lamp. "These destructive cells [in the good eye]
should clear up a few days after we have done the
enucleation," he muttered. And then he added:
"If we're not too late!"

As I was being wheeled into the operation
theater, I asked, "Have they ever taken out the
wrong eye?"

"Yes, that has happened," the nurse responded, "but there's not much chance of it hap-
pening anymore. There is a big X on your fore-
head over the eye that is to be removed. They will
get the correct one."

Dr. Payne replaced the right eye with a golden
ball about the same size. The muscles of the eye
were sewn to the ball so that the ball would move
in the socket just as the natural eyeball had. The
"glass eye" is only a thin cap that is slipped
under the eyelid so that it rests on the membrane
that covers the ball. When the golden ball moves

from one side to the other, the cap also moves, giving the appearance of being a natural eye.

My prosthesis was so natural looking that when I returned to Binghamton, New York, where we made our furloughs, my friends couldn't tell which was the real eye and which was the "wooden one" as I called it. "Bill, which one is your plastic eye?" they would ask. My customary reply was, "It's the one with the kind look."

As the days turned into weeks after the enucleation, I was haunted by Dr. Payne's last statement: "If we're not too late!" I was beginning to wonder if it really was too late. Great halos surrounded lights at night, vision was poor in the daytime, and there was discomfort even though I constantly used eyedrops. Maybe Satan was about to permanently disable one of those bothersome translators after all!

One day, as I stepped into the office of one of our leaders, he had very exciting news for me. "Bill, I have just received a very interesting letter from an old man in Canada. This is the gist of his letter: 'I have a list of missionaries for whom I pray each day. One of them is Bill Cutts. A few days ago as I was praying, I prayed for Cutts and went on to the next name on my list. The Lord said, "Go back to Cutts." I dutifully prayed longer for him, then returned to my list. Once again, the Lord told me, "Go back to Cutts!" I had no idea what Cutts's problem was, but I stayed with that name until I had assurance from heaven that my prayer had been heard and that God had taken care of Cutts's problem.' "

I believe that my present vision—as good as it was 60 years ago—is the result of the fervent, intercessory praying of that dear brother in Christ.

22

Softened Up

THE OPENING MONTHS of 1965 reminded me of a military action that softens up a resistant area by simultaneously dropping bombs and shelling the area from a warship off the coast. Still home on furlough, I was saving money—or so I thought—by driving to a nearby farm to purchase milk instead of buying it in the store. One evening as I hurried out of the house with a gallon jug in each hand I slipped and fell on an ice-covered concrete slab outside the door. There was excruciating pain in my right hip.

It was discovered that my hip bone was broken off at the ball, very near the socket, making it difficult for the surgeon to line it up properly for splicing it back together. However, two weeks after the surgery I had graduated from a walker and was doing pretty well on crutches. One evening, while a nurse was attempting to roll me over in bed, I felt pain and said, "It won't go any further that way."

She cheerfully replied, "Of course it will," and gave me a push. The push displaced the broken pieces that the surgeon had spliced with what is called a Ken Nail. I was scheduled for a second operation the following day.

The second splicing job held together and I was mobile. I had been home from the hospital for only a short time, when one afternoon Amy came home from kindergarten crying. There was an epidemic of mumps at her school and she was feeling wretched. I put her on my lap and kissed her, trying to offset her miseries.

Two mornings later I discovered a bump under my jaw as I was shaving. Not only one, but two! The mumps lowered my body resistance enough to allow the malaria in my system to flare up. The combined illnesses lit the fuse which set off another attack of iritis. High fever produced delirium.

The malaria soon responded to medication and eventually the discomfort from the mumps subsided. The iritis in my good eye cleared up and I was feeling quite at ease getting about on my crutches. I had missed going on the fall missionary deputation tour, but now I told the Society that I felt I was ready to go on the spring tour as long as someone met me at trains and buses to help carry my suitcases.

It was during this time that I received a letter from one of our colleagues working in Irian Jaya. The letter stated in part: "Bill, the Word tells us: 'Faithful are the wounds of a friend.' I hope that some day you will be able to forgive me, but for your own good I have written to our headquarters strongly urging them not to send you back to the field."

At Council, the annual general meeting of The Christian and Missionary Alliance, headquarters officials set up a meeting to discuss my case. It was a grave, somber session. When I was asked to state my opinion, I told them that because of all the things I had had to do, very little of the Bible had been translated into the Moni language. I explained that on the field there were no other missionaries to the Monis who would be able to carry on translation work. I reminded them of the impossibilty of the Moni church being born and becoming strong apart from having God's Word on which to feed. I recounted why I was certain my Lord had called me to give them His Word in writing and explained that I could return to the field unafraid. I was confident that the One who called me had the power to keep me going.

No one spoke.

Dr. Kroh finally broke the silence. "If it were me, I would go back."

There was nothing else to be said. The meeting was over.

The following morning at a full session of Council with about 2,000 people present, I was asked to lead in the opening prayer and to read the Scripture. Dr. King, president of the Alliance was presiding, and he spoke to the assembly: "This man who made his way to the podium on crutches has every possible reason for not return-ing to the field. But he is going back in spite of everything because he trusts his Lord." He made an appeal to those who had no excuse for staying in the homeland to commit their lives to the Lord for whatever He might call them to do.

" 'If my people would but listen to me,/ if Israel would follow my ways,/ how quickly would I subdue their enemies/ and turn my hand against their foes! . . . But you would be fed with the finest of wheat;/ with honey from the rock I would satisfy you' " (Psalm 81:13–14, 16).

23

No Good Thing...

O N OUR FIRST FURLOUGH a reputable physician told us there was very little hope that Gracie would ever conceive a child, and if she did, only the most expert care would ensure the birth of a live, healthy baby. The officials at Alliance headquarters were sufficiently convinced of the accuracy of the prognosis that they eventually granted us permission to adopt up to two children to be on regular mission allowance.

It was true that many years earlier Gracie had been ruled out as ever being a biological mother, but as a result of the mumps, I now had slim chance of being a biological father. About May 1968, when Gracie was 44 years old, I was 53 and we had been married for 21 years, the time arrived for the demonstration that nothing is too hard for our God.

Gracie began to be bothered with unusual symptoms of persistent nausea. She thought that she had some type of flu. The field conference was coming up, so she was looking forward to having a medical checkup at that time.

Gracie was examined by Dr. Thelma Becroft of the Australian Baptist Missionary Society as soon as an appointment could be arranged. She felt a lump in Gracie's abdomen and exclaimed, "What have we here? Have you felt life at any time, Gracie?"

"No."

"Well then, don't get too excited or breathe a word about it so that you won't be embarrassed. It could be a tumor. We must keep checking on it."

Gracie tried to be obedient, but she was pretty sure it was not a tumor. One evening, during a testimony meeting at the conference, Gracie stood up and made her famous birth announcement: "Bless the Lord, O my soul, and *all that is within me*, bless His holy name."

Dr. Becroft advised Gracie to have the baby in Irian Jaya, but I felt that we should consider the doctor's advice in 1952—that if ever she became pregnant, only the most expert care could bring a live, healthy baby into the world. It would be fine with me if "William Albert Cutts, Jr." had my hair and two eyes the same color as my one, but I was determined to prevent his having a body like mine.

Dr. Becroft arranged for us to go to the hospital in beautiful Goroka, Papua New Guinea, which is in the interior highlands about the same altitude as Hitadipa. At that time the most expert medical personnel in Australia took turns with a stint at the government hospital in Goroka. There was no way to ascertain when the baby would be born. Dr. Becroft said, "We'll just have to pull a date out of a hat." When we arrived in Goroka we thought we were about a month early.

The Summer Institute of Linguistics people invited us to come to Ukarumpa, a town about 15 minutes' flying time from Goroka for the waiting period. The SIL translators all have houses with modern conveniences at Ukarumpa. Each translator lives under very primitive conditions with the tribe whose language he or she is translating. After several months, having gathered reams of material, they return to Ukarumpa to process it. We thoroughly enjoyed our stay with them—the refreshing fellowship and the opportunity to discuss my translation problems with experts.

The gynecologist who examined Gracie upon our arrival at Goroka told us to be back there at a certain date for the birth. Dr. Ross had confirmed the prognosis of 1952: a natural birth could be very dangerous. "This little one is too precious to take a chance. I will do a Caesarian section."

It was a beautiful evening as I sat on the veranda waiting for our baby and praying. I didn't have too long to wait, for soon a small white blanket bearing "William Albert, Jr." appeared. Elation, joy, thanksgiving, praise and worship filled my mind simultaneously as the tiny bundle was placed in my lap. "You have a little girl. Would you like to hold her until we get your wife cleaned up?"

It had never occurred to us that our baby might be a girl!

In order to get back into Irian Jaya, we had to

send our passport to the American Consul in Jakarta together with a certificate of birth from Goroka and a photo. I brought my camera to photograph the new baby. Now we had to decide on a name for this little sweetheart. Eventually we agreed that the traits we sought—beauty, cadence, euphony, harmony—were implicit in the name Faith Elizabeth.

And that is not the end of the story. Thirteen months later we were back in Goroka going through the same routine. This time we returned to Irian Jaya with William Albert Cutts, Jr.

Many letters came addressed to "Abraham and Sarah Cutts, Hitadipa." Ten-year-old Amy had a dormmate at the missionary kids' school at Sentani who observed, "When these missionaries find out that they can have babies, they keep having them and having them!"

"For the Lord God is a sun and shield;/ the Lord bestows favor and honor;/ no good thing does he withold/ from those whose walk is blameless" (Psalm 84:11).

24

Isa Sabo

WHEN GRACIE AND I ARRIVED in Moni land in December 1950, we found a staunch ally in the gospel. Through Ken Troutman's ministry, a Moni chief named Kiguabi had been healed of asthma, and because of that, he was the friend of the missionaries. He was the one who saved our lives in those early days by reminding his people of the old prophecy that one day *hazi* would come out of the west and perhaps Gracie and I were the very ones who would fulfill that prophecy.

Kiguabi had four sons, two of whom were young men when we went to Homeyo. One of his sons was Timu Nggaga Bega (Night Bird) and the oldest son was Isa Sabo, which translated would be Ekari Skirt. Both of the older boys helped us learn the Moni language, but Isa Sabo, who was a very clever fellow and had all the characteristics for becoming a great chief, was especially helpful. He was an exceptionally handsome young man, very outgoing and friendly. Though he was married and had a little boy, he informed me, "I love Jesus, but I love girls too."

In 1950 there was a high bride payment price.

123

Usually a young man could not marry a beautiful young girl because he could not come up with sufficient cowrie shells. Frequently the young men had to settle for old widows.

The men all slept in the men's house of a village. But when a man took a wife, he would build a house and fence off a garden space for her to tend. He would also give her some piglets. Each wife's house was occupied by the woman, her daughters until they reached marriageable age and her sons until they were about six years old. Then the boys went to live with their father in the men's house. The wife also kept the pigs in her house. To avoid a beating, it behooved the woman to make sure that all the pigs were in their corner of the house at night.

A wife raised her assigned pigs by growing food for them in her assigned garden. When they were mature, the husband would trade the pork for cowrie shells, eventually accumulating enough to buy a second bride. By the time a man had reached middle age he would have the right shells to enter the competition to buy the prettiest young girl in town. She would then be the recipient of the most affection from the husband, a situation which produced bitter jealousy among the members of the harem.

Isa Sabo's father, being an important chief, was able to circumvent the usual procedure for a young man's acquiring a wife and had started his oldest son out with a beautiful young woman. She had given birth to a boy—a very important thing to do if a woman wanted to earn the favor of her husband. Isa Sabo adored the little boy who was about five years old when we went to Homeyo.

The nationals' huts are built by driving sharpened slats into the ground, then tying horizontal slats to them, usually two walls with grass stuffed between them for insulation against the cold. The floor is made by tying numerous small poles together side by side and covering them with woven bamboo. Round poles are tied above the structure to form a roof with a proper pitch so that the rain will run off. Tree bark and grass are then laid on the poles and secured. The huts are built low—no one can stand upright in them—and firewood is kept dry and ready for use by placing it on a rack suspended from the roof directly over the hearth in the center of the floor area.

There is only one doorway in a native hut and the door is a rather complicated arrangement of wooden slats in channels at the bottom and top of the opening. It takes a bit of doing to get all the slats lined up properly to keep out the night air and opening the door in the morning is much more complicated than turning a door knob.

One night, while everyone was asleep in Isa Sabo's wife's hut, fire somehow reached the dry wood slats that made up the door. They awakened to find the single doorway burning with intense heat. By the time the villagers heard the women's screams, the whole hut was a blazing inferno. Isa Sabo and his fellow villagers stood by helplessly listening to the screams of the burning women and his little son and the squealing of the doomed pigs.

The next morning we were told that Isa Sabo was beside himself with grief and talked of committing suicide by jumping into the nearby Kemabu River. I rushed to his side to try to comfort him, actually gripping his wrist to restrain him from running to the river. Of course, he could have easily broken away from my grip, but he later gave me credit for saving his life by hanging on to him. We were close friends. It was Isa Sabo and his family who had moved to the Dugindoga Valley with us and helped with translation and the construction of the air field.

There was a lot of confusion connected with the old tribal custom of killing pigs when people died. Some Christians thought that it was all right to kill pigs after a death as a means of comforting the living family members. But the new *bazi* talk that had come from the Ilaga stated that Christians were to have nothing to do with the custom.

It was on such an occasion that Isa Sabo got himself into real trouble. A man was dying. The new Christians around him were urging him to leave this life praying to Jesus and trusting the Lord to take him safely to heaven. But he wanted someone to kill a pig and cook it just as he was departing so that he could see the smoke ascending and climb skyward on it. No one would think of granting the old man's request; that is, no one except Isa Sabo.

The community leaders immediately came to me with their ultimatum: "Look here, Tuani. You are teaching us how to walk on the *bazi* trail and your son is doing exactly the opposite of what you are teaching us to do. Either fire him immediately or go back to Homeyo because if you keep him on as your right-hand man, none of us will listen to you anymore."

Isa Sabo tried to convince me that in his mind he had not thought of going back to any form of the old spirit appeasement practice, but was merely granting the last wish of a dying man. I explained to him that in the eyes of the infant church he had committed an unpardonable blunder and that since the Lord had called me to come to the new area to help establish His church, I had no alternative but to part company with him.

The handsome, disarming smile was replaced by a pair of eyes that struck fear to my heart. It seemed I was looking into the eyes of a demoniac.

One day, as Isa Sabo was working in his garden on the steep sides of the riverbank, he saw a woman working far below him. He dislodged a huge boulder which thundered down the slope on its way to the river. It crashed through the fence separating the two gardens, narrowly missing the woman. We heard too that Isa Sabo frequently beat his new wife unmercifully, even striking her with the blade of an axe.

After that, Isa Sabo acted like a schizophrenic. Yet he regularly attended the church services, singing the gospel songs louder than anyone else.

One Sunday, while Pendeta Ototome was giving the message, he thought of a Bible verse he wanted to read and stopped to find it. By that time, quite a bit of the New Testmanet had been translated and mimeographed. Each portion was printed as a separate booklet. As Oto continued his search, there was a lengthy pause and Isa Sabo impatiently demanded, "Let's get this over with; we want to go home."

I admonished him, "It's not good to do that to the preacher. You will get him confused."

Isa Sabo sat there without making further comment, but the instant the benediction was pronounced, he ran out of the building. He returned shortly with his bow and arrows. He sat in the doorway of the church and announced that I had been the fly in his ointment long enough and that he was going to kill me in a few minutes. Gracie carried the little ones to where Isa Sabo was sitting, asking his permission to let them go home in order for her to take care of their needs. Bill Jr. was only a few months old and Faith was about 16 months. Zani Mala and Amy were at boarding school at Sentani. He moved aside to let her pass. Then he looked at me. "It's not good for me to kill you here in the house of the Chief of the Sky," he said. "Let's go to your front yard."

As the two of us sat in a corner of the yard, he made sure that our conversation wouldn't be disturbed by hurling rocks at anyone that ventured too close. Talking crazily, he suggested that our former close friendship might be restored if we

went to a brighter, fairer land. "I will kill you," he
said. "Then your friends will kill me and we can
go to heaven together." Finally he said, "Sunday
is not a good day to kill people, so I will wait until
tomorrow. If you promise to give me anything I
ask, I might not kill you."

"How can I promise to give you what you ask
without first hearing what you want?"

He finally left, assuring me that he would return
in the morning. Gracie had gone to our upstairs
bedroom with the little ones and had been praying the whole time. I went to the two-way radio.
One by one I turned the channels and announced, "This is Hitadipa. We have an emergency. Is anyone standing by?"

It was thrilling to hear a voice coming from the
speaker. "MAF Sentani is reading you, Bill.
What's your problem?"

I reported what had been taking place and men-
tioned Isa Sabo's promise of return the next
morning. I asked if someone could drive to Jayapura and alert the Alliance missionaries to pray
for us. He promised to get word to our people.

Early next morning someone came to our
house to report that my potential executioner had
been seen carefully sharpening a knife. I wondered which of the two weapons—knife or arrow—
would be the least painful for my demise.

Eventually Isa Sabo arrived with his weapons
and ordered me to get mine in order to avoid any
adverse publicity that might arise if he shot an
unarmed person. When I told him that I didn't

own any, he said, "Then I'll go home and get you some," adding a sinister, "I'll be back."

While he was gone, I returned to the radio to inform our colleagues that the next half hour would be critical and asked them to support us in earnest prayer.

When Isa Sabo returned, I invited him to come up on the veranda to talk things over. He said, "Sit down."

I replied, "There are two chairs here. You sit in one and I will sit in the other."

The second time he snarled, "Sit down."

Again I repeated the invitation for him to be seated first. For the third time he yelled, "Sit down," and struck me on the chest with his fist.

I breathed a prayer to my Lord and with both hands grabbed the fist that had struck me, holding on for dear life. What neither Isa Sabo nor I had noticed was that a group of my national friends had been creeping up closer and closer to the porch. At the instant I grabbed his fist, two men leaped onto the porch and grabbed the other. They put him face down on the floor and held him while I went to the shack to get a chain, some heavy wire, and a pair of pliers. After chaining his hands behind his back, we let him up.

Isa Sabo stood on the porch and made his defense to the large crowd that had gathered on the lawn. He said that he, an innocent man, had his life ruined by this missionary who left the straight and narrow way and who became a thorough-going rascal. Meanwhile, I got to the two-way radio, reported how my Lord had answered prayer and asked for an MAF plane to come in and take him to the prison at Nabire.

Pilot Dave Hoisington reported that he was in the area and would drop his load at Beoga and come over. Isa Sabo was loaded into the plane screaming like a trussed pig.

Dave watched him yelling out threats and straining at his fetters. "Bill," he said, "I have a feeling that I shouldn't do this. If he gets loose, it will be the end of me and the plane. I think I will go back to the Beoga and get Don Gibbons to sit with him and restrain him if he gets loose."

Dave's hunch was right. By working constantly with his fetters, Isa Sabo was able to wear out the wire that secured the chain on one wrist. He walked up and down the airstrip waving his arms—with the chain still dangling from one of them—and shouting, "God has broken my shackle. As soon as I get my other arm free, I'll come up to your house and whip you with this chain."

By this time, I was in no danger. The grapevine worked better than telephone systems. I had only one enemy but hundreds of friends who gathered ready to use whatever restraining methods might be necessary. Knowing that they might not be too gentle, Isa Sabo kept his distance. Later on, as night was falling, a group of Danis insisted on sleeping on our screened-in front porch without any shield from the cold night breezes.

It wasn't long until we heard the drone of the

Cessna 185 and Dave rolled up our airstrip with Don on board. Isa Sabo invited him to his hut for a chat. "Why did you want to kill Tuani Cutts?" Don asked.

Isa Sabo replied, "I wanted to kill him because he is not fit to live. He has translated nearly all of the *hazi* talk into our language—everything that is of no importance—but has deliberately left out the parts that tell us how to get the things that he has!" These ideas come from a powerful expectation that is prevalent throughout the whole island—a belief that has been a hindrance to the reception of the gospel. It is called a "cargo cult." Promoters of the cult teach that the mountains are full of treasures such as the things owned by the western missionaries. These missionaries have the keys to the treasure chambers and help themselves freely, selfishly keeping the keys out of the hands of the nationals. Rumor had it that there was a passageway under our house and that after we locked our doors for the night and turned off the lights, we went to get the things we needed.

Don knew that it would be extremely difficult for me to cope with Isa Sabo's presence on our station. So he offered him a number of axe heads and transportation for his earthly possessions if he would burn down his house and go back to Homeyo to live. This is what he did.

Some years later, Gracie and I offered to make a few visits to Homeyo during the year that the resident missionaries were on furlough. We tended to matters pertaining to the station, paid the wages of station laborers, and also held seminars for the national workers of the area. Isa Sabo attended. We were told that his wife had become blind and couldn't leave her hut—possibly as a result of the head injuries inflicted by her husband. She was unable to go to the garden to get food for herself, so her husband was letting her starve to death.

During one seminar, Isa Sabo raised the subject of a pension from our mission for all the hard work he had done while he was in Hitadipa. He was told by the national pastors to keep quiet, that the assembly had more important things to talk about. I was amazed to see the formerly powerful, proud, fearless leader meekly close his mouth and do what he was told.

His last months on earth were spent in agony. An arrow tip from an old war wound had dislodged in his chest, producing acute pain with every move he made. This one who knew more scripture than almost anyone else in his tribe, who "loved Jesus, but loved girls too," this one also came to the end of the trail.

"Therefore everyone who hears these words of mine and puts them into practice is like a wise man who built his house on the rock. The rain came down, the streams rose, and the winds blew and beat against that house; yet it did not fall, because it had its foundation on the rock. But everyone who hears these words of mine and does not put them into practice is like a foolish man who built his house on sand. The rain came down, the streams rose, and the winds blew and beat against that house, and it fell with a great crash" (Matthew 7:24–27).

25

Ototome

OTOTOME, A YOUNG MONI MAN from the Dugindoga Valley was visiting the Beoga Valley, being entertained in the home of one of the locals. Just as a guest in the States might help the hostess by drying the dishes, Ototome went to the woods to get some firewood. There he was struck on the back by a falling tree. He later told us that his back had been broken. The new Christian Damals who were with him said, "No problem. We'll pray for you and the Chief of Heaven will answer our prayers and heal you." They prayed and Ototome got up and walked back to the hut.

"What sort of thing is this new talk about the Chief of Heaven and His Son?" he wondered. "It has power—not at all like our spirit-appeasement ceremonies where we give all that we have and get nothing in return."

While Ototome was still in the Beoga, messengers came to tell him that his little son had contracted diarrhea and was getting weaker and weaker. Again, the new Damal Christians said, "Don't get upset. The Chief of Heaven has power to heal your boy. We will pray for him right now and he will be well again.''

Ototome immediately headed home with the messengers, trekking as fast as possible, hoping to see his son still alive. He was amazed when he saw the boy, not lying listlessly in his mother's lap, but out in the village yard playing with friends. Just as the Beoga Christians had prayed. The news of this double miracle spread through the Dugindoga Valley like wildfire.

When Gracie and I moved there, one of the first people we met was Ototome. Just about everyone was hungry for *hazi*, but Ototome was especially zealous to learn more perfectly the ways of the Chief of the Sky and to take them to others. He was also one of the very few who had only one wife. Most men were polygamists.

I remember one Sunday baptizing a chief and all five of his wives at the same time. He and two of the women locked arms so that a helper and I could immerse them together. Then the three remaining wives locked arms and were baptized.

Baptizing polygamists was one thing, but setting them apart to preach the gospel was quite another. We said to Ototome, ''Oto, in the written Word of the Chief of Heaven we are told that the man who divides the *hazi* talk must be the husband of only one wife. Almost everyone in the Dugindoga has more than one wife. You are one of the few exceptions. Perhaps the Chief of Heaven has kept you from marrying another so that you can be a worker for Him. Are you willing for that?''

"I am truly happy to do that. I will go to your school until His Word has been carefully planted in my stomach, and then I will walk all over this area dividing His Word with those who have not heard it.''

School was not easy for Ototome. Like many other Monis, he could see a bird in the branches of a tree half a mile away, but trying to differentiate between the shapes of letters was misery. The primers that Gracie and I had prepared used the Frank Laubach method of pictures to represent letters.

When Ototome was a young boy, he and his friends had a mock war using sharpened darts and one of Oto's eyes had stopped a dart, adding to his reading difficulties. However, Oto desperately wanted to be a good gospel worker, and where there is a will, there is usually a way.

Ototome replaced Isa Sabo as my translation helper. Working on the translation of the New Testament with me, combined with his attendance at the Bible school, caused him to grow quickly in the knowledge of God. Many times I heard him praying for the fullness of the Holy Spirit in his life. His sermons soon began to take on a depth that made them different from those of his fellow national pastors.

Oto had been a pastor for only a short time when his colleagues recognized his godly life and requested that he be ordained, conferring upon him the title Pendeta. Soon after his ordination, Pendeta Ototome was elected district superintendent—Ketua Klasis—of the Dugindoga. They called him Klasis for short. Few have done as well as Oto in carrying out their responsibilities. He felt that as district superintendent he should regularly visit every church in his district. For Oto, that meant going over long, difficult trails, often in unpopulated areas. Sometimes he became ill, despairing of his life, but even though frail and subject to frightening attacks of asthma, he was always ready to head out to another village.

The time came when it was thought best for Pendeta Ototome to step down from being district superintendent. No one in the district was more godly than he; the problem was that he was only semiliterate and knew no Indonesian. KINGMI— The Alliance National Church of Irian Jaya—had come into being, the daughter of the larger Alliance church of Indonesia. There were large conferences on the national level where everything that went into Oto's ears or came out of his mouth had to go through an interpreter. Another duty of the district superintendent was to represent the church before the Department of Religion, and Oto's ignorance of the national trade language was a definite handicap.

Ototome accepted this with an attitude of true spiritual maturity. He was his Lord's completely dedicated servant in every way, and it did not matter to him whether he was on the podium in the place of honor or sitting in a pew being fed by a brother in Christ. Pendeta Ototome was truly a trophy of grace in whom the Spirit of God had made His home.

26

Second Timothy

THE PRINCIPAL OF THE MONI Bible school was standing on the platform giving his testimony in the Bible school auditorium. The purpose of these meetings was to give budding pastors practice in conducting church services and to afford those in the homiletics class an opportunity to try their wings. The principal was dressed in neat, clean clothing complete with necktie. It was a compliment to the Maranatha Bible School to have such a sharp-looking, well-educated young man as their principal. His name was Yahya Wea—not a Moni name. He was a member of the Wano tribe, which lived in the general area of the Dugindoga Valley.

Yahya had worked for us a few years prior to this. We selected him, not because of his physical stature, but because he was weak and emaciated and we wanted to make sure that he received the kind of food and vitamins that would build up his body. Yahya was a soft-spoken young man, always eager to please us in whatever job we gave him to do. Besides working in our house, he was also a full-time student in the Bible school.

We noted early that Yahya was a very clever

young man. He quickly bridged the language barrier between his native Wano and Moni, the language in which the Bible school operated. Other
nationals had been my helpers, but Yahya quickly
learned to do everything I showed him—he even
learned to use my electric drill. As my strength
diminished, one job that was particularly annoy-
ing to me was the maintenance of our freshwater
supply line. Whereas our first station, Homeyo,
had adequate rainfall, the new station at Hitadipa
was very dry. We frequently had to have water
carried from the river and there was not even a
remote hope that we could ever have an indoor
toilet.

One day, however, some nationals told me that
there was a spring up the side of a steep mountain
behind our house. I investigated, found their report to be true, and ordered 300 feet of garden
hose from Australia. The result was water in great
abundance for all of our needs. But maintaining
the line was time-consuming because the hose
was constantly sucking up little stones from the
spring and there was a persistent root-system
growing inside it at the upper end.

I took Yahya up the hill with me several times,
and showed him how to diagnose the cause of
the stoppage and make the necessary repairs. It
wasn't long before I could say, "Our water isn't
running. Will you get it going for me?" Yahya
became to us what Timothy was to Paul.

Not only was Yahya my right-hand man, but
soon he was able to give his people some of the

Word of God in their mother tongue. It was at this time that other Wanos on our station begged Gracie to put some of the words of the Chief of Heaven into their language. Yahya was the instrument by which this could be accomplished for he was a fluent reader in Moni and as Gracie and he read the Moni Scriptures, Yahya would tell her the equivalent in his tribal tongue. The Wano language had not been reduced to writing, so Yahya and Gracie worked out a Wano alphabet his people would be able to read. As they worked together, the four Gospels, a song book, the catechism and primers materialized for the jubilant Wanos.

In his student days, Yahya was one of the best students in the homiletics class and delivered sermons that were well organized and instructive. He was frequently asked to speak in the church at Hitadipa and often trekked to outlying villages to preach the good news.

As I listened to his testimony that night I remembered the time, half a dozen years before, when a group of about 20 young people walked into the Hitadipa station telling us that they were from the Wano tribe, which lived in the lowlands to the northeast. They said they had heard about the Chief of Heaven and about His Son who came to this earth and died so that people could live forever. They had heard that a school had been opened at Hitadipa and had felt a strange leading to leave their homeland and come to see if it was really true. Their leader had even left his dying mother behind in his village, so peristent was the call.

It hadn't been easy for them to adapt to life in Hitadipa. There was the language barrier as well as the need to build houses and plant gardens to sustain themselves. But they were very industrious and determined to learn all they could in the Bible school and then return to their tribe.

One day their leader became ill and was unable to leave his hut. Until that time no nurse had been appointed to our station, so I had taken on the job. I would report pulse rates, temperatures and general symptoms of the sick to a mission doctor on the two-way radio. The doctor would attempt to diagnose the illness and prescribe medication that would hopefully help the patient recover. In this case, as always, I carefully followed the doctor's orders, but my Wano patient became progressively worse and slipped into a coma.

Over the two-way radio, I pleaded with the doctor to okay an emergency flight to bring him to the hospital. "Doctor, this patient is a special case. He is the leader of a group of people from a tribe to our northeast. We have never contacted them, but God Himself led them to us. We must do whatever we can to save this young man's life. Please let me send him to you."

"Bill," replied the doctor, "I hear you and am ever so sorry that I can't help you. It is too late to send him now. If you order a plane to put him on, he will be dead before he gets to me."

"But," he continued, "there is one thing that you could try. There is only one chance in a million that it will work, but that is better than no chance at all. Fill a hot water bottle with water. Add some sugar and a bit of salt. Hang it on the wall beside him about a foot higher than his body. Introduce the hose into him rectally and leave it hooked up day and night."

The patient continued comatose that day and the next day and the next. I could detect no breathing nor could I find any pulse. But obviously he had not died, for there was neither the ashen pallor of death nor rigor mortis. The young Wanos and the Moni Christians joined in earnest prayer that the Chief of Heaven would display His mighty power and raise up their fallen friend.

Long days of anxious waiting dragged by as the little band quietly prayed and wept. About the seventh day of the coma, someone touched his toe with a hot coal from the hearth to see if he was still alive. There was no reaction. Their young leader must be dead!

As the young women sat in the hut mourning their loss, the young men gathered a huge pile of wood for his funeral pyre. Entering the hut to carry out his corpse, they took a final look at his face. One eye was open! Soon his other eye opened!

Now, before our eyes, the principal of the Maranatha Bible School stood before the congregation that midweek night, smiling, as he told the story of the comatose Wano leader—the story I have just recounted. Then he concluded, "I was that young man!"

27

Toward the Goal

" **H**OW DO YOU PLAN TO OPERATE a Bible school without a Bible?"

Perhaps Irian Jaya was the land of the first Bibleless Bible school, for the school which Gracie and I started was indeed that. A student enrolling at the school could not purchase a Moni Bible at the local bookstore. But as his course progressed, his "Bible" grew in size. When the classes were over for the day, Peterus Holombau (Alice in Wonderland's husband), Pendeta Ototome and I translated pages of whatever Bible passage would be needed for the next day's lesson.

Before we got our mimeograph machine with its permanent black copies of the stencils, we used a gelatin duplicator that made fairly legible purple copies from a master sheet. There was just one problem—classes were held outdoors and after a few hours of direct sunlight, the "Bibles" faded to white sheets of blank paper!

By the end of our fifth term on the field, Gracie and the national teachers were taking on most of the teaching load. That allowed my two translation helpers and me to keep plugging away at the work of getting the New Testament into their language. But it was not a simple task.

There are many things in the Scriptures that do not exist in Moni land. Ships, rudders, anchors and sails are unknown, as are horses with their bridles and bits. Most Monis have never seen a cow or sheep, though in recent years some missionaries own them. Gold, silver and the precious stones of the Revelation are unknown to them as are lions, bears, foxes and whales. They can only guess what happens in summer and winter. There is no problem with east and west since the sun rises and sets in those places, but the concept of north and south is another matter. They have over 20 varieties of sweet potatoes, each with its separate name, but colors have never been considered important enough to assign special names. If we count white as a color, they have names for three: white, light and dark. As you can imagine, this poses great problems for the translator when he or she comes to the story of a purple robe being put on the Lord Jesus.

Basically, their counting is only to five. They count one, two, three, four, five on one hand, then one to five on the other hand, on one foot and on the other foot. Then they say "all of one man" or "all of two men." The number 73 would be expressed as "all of three men, three on the foot of another man." But at this point, entering the realm of "higher mathematics," they suggest that we write: "Very many; to count it is bad."

We gradually got some inkling of how to translate into the Moni language items foreign to it. When the nationals saw chickens for the first time they exclaimed, *"Bega wogo."* Literally translated, this would be "bird pig." In their thinking, the word *pig* means an edible, domesticated something, in this case, a bird. We learned later that we could name a foreign, inedible animal by using the Indonesian word for the animal in combination with the Moni word for dog. For precious stones we used the Indonesian name prefixed by "a stone that people treasure by the name of . . . ."

The Ekaris call their canoes *koma.* The Monis who live near the Ekaris call the canoes *du koma* or "water vehicle" because the Moni word for water is *du. Wulu, wulu, wulu* is the sound that a plane makes as it flies overhead, so an airplane is a *wulu koma.* Earth in Moni is *mai,* so an automobile is a *mai koma.*

One day, in order to get a word for *anchor,* I told my men to pretend that we were in a huge *du koma* in deep water. Having fastened one end of a rope to my chair, I tied the other end to a heavy metal object and dropped it on the floor. The word I got was quite simple—a pig-tethering device with the word *koma* substituted for pig. For many unknown terms, we described what the item does. A prophet has a long name in Moni: "A man who divides the word that God said to him, 'Speak.'"

The United Bible Societies have developed a Shorter Old Testament, in size roughly half that of the complete Old Testament. Gracie continued to translate this into Moni when other duties allowed. At the same time, my two helpers and I turned out book after book of the New Testament. The almost unreadable sheets of paper turned into stencils on my manual Olympia wide-carriage typewriter. Each stencil turned into hundreds of pages on our Gestetner duplicator. And after we had trained a number of nationals to do it, the pages turned into booklets on an assembly table, at first in our dining room and later in the bookstore. Longer books, such as one of the Gospels or the Revelation, each became a separate mimeographed booklet. Several short epistles were combined to make a booklet. There were 13 separate booklets in the Moni New Testament.

It took a bit of doing for a Moni pastor to preach from his New Testament. He could prepare a sermon by placing several books in order, with book markers in each. But woe betide him if, in the middle of a sermon, he wished to find a text in one of the other booklets in his net, or maybe in his house. When the pastors went over the trail to distant churches it would have been fairly simple to keep a single book dry, but a different matter to keep a whole stack of them from getting rained on. They looked at our English-language Bibles and said, "We would love to have a little book like you have with all the books of the Bible under one cover."

Granting their request became our greatest desire. In order to accomplish this, a gargantuan task had to be completed. The United Bible Societies have a long list of requirements if they are to do the printing. A major one is the correlating of parallel passages in the four Gospels. During the many years the translating of each of the Gospels took, we had found different ways of saying the same thing, had changed the spelling of names, etc. The result was that a passage in Matthew was different in Moni from the identical passage in Luke. Another Society requirement was to make sure that nothing had been omitted in preparing the manuscript for printing, necessitating a couple of readers, one in Moni and the other in English, to carefully read every word. It became quite obvious that there would not be enough time to finish the job during the remainder of the time left in our sixth term. However, we were confident that what we purposed doing was our Lord's will and that He would give us the strength to remain on the field until the undertaking was completed.

28

More Fusillades

IT WAS REMINISCENT of 85-year-old Caleb presenting his credentials to Joshua. "I want Mount Hebron to be my possession. Not only did God say that it would be mine, but I'm fully able to drive out those giants that live there. I'm as strong now as I was 45 years ago when I came here as one of the 12 spies."

The scene was the 1979 field conference in Irian Jaya. Alliance missionaries normally retire at age 65. Gracie and I had been on the field for six terms and I would reach retiral age in a few weeks. I was asking my colleagues to vote favorably so that we could get authorization from headquarters in Nyack, New York, to return to the field for a seventh term because our task was not yet completed. We had prepared the gift for the Moni tribe, but we desired, as it were, to tie it up in lovely wrapping paper with a ribbon and a beautiful bow.

Before we left conference, I asked our field chairman, John Ellenberger, if he could divulge the results of the voting. "Yes, Bill. The field wants you and Gracie to return and finish the job of getting the Moni Bible ready for printing."

Now, it was the summer of 1983. Gracie and her translation helpers were making good progress on translating the Shorter Old Testament. My two helpers and I were well along in the revision of the New Testament. The Bible school was running nicely with very little help from either of us. Not only did we have national teachers who were doing a good job with the teaching load, but we also had a national principal. We would leave the field for the last time in May 1985, and it appeared that both the Shorter Old Testament and the complete New Testament would be ready for printing before we left. All seemed once again to be clear sailing.

Then, one morning Gracie noticed a numbness in her arms. We weren't too concerned at first, but the numbness kept spreading up her arms and then her legs. It was decided that she should go to the mission hospital at Mulia, about half an hour's flying distance east of Hitadipa. This was the Unevangelized Fields Mission hospital operated by Dr. Jerry Powell. Dr. Powell made the most thorough tests he could with his limited equipment and concluded that there was some sort of chemical imbalance in her body. Even though Gracie was taking all the medications prescribed, the numbness continued to spread.

Our field doctors take a very dim view of missionaries laying down their lives on the fields. If there is any question about anyone's ability to pull through the illness, plans are made to get him or her back home. Thus, there was serious discussion that we should immediately head for the States. However, the mission doctors agreed that Gracie should go first to Penang, Malaysia, for tests, and if these turned out to be inconclusive, she should proceed to Singapore.

Gracie was greatly relieved to learn that our Lord had provided a travelling companion for her—not an ordinary companion, but a registered nurse. Ben and Ruth Karcesky were fellow Alliance missionaries working with us in Irian Jaya. Their son Nathan required surgery before school started in Malaysia, so he and Ruth were scheduled to fly out early. Faith was about to return to high school in Penang and decided to travel with Mom and the Karceskys.

Gracie's many tests in the hospital at Penang didn't throw any more light on the cause for the numbness than Dr. Powell's. So it was on to Singapore. Gracie was assigned to a Chinese neurosurgeon who did everything he could to diagnose the cause of her problem. At the conclusion of the tests, he announced: "As to the cause of your numbness, the tests have been inconclusive. But this could be very dangerous. You must pack your things as soon as you arrive back in Irian Jaya and return to the States immediately."

But even while the doctor was telling Gracie the bad news, our sovereign God was revealing to him that he had said the wrong thing. The following morning he returned. "On second thought, I suggest that you go back to your work and keep in close touch with your mission doctors. If there is no change, continue to work as you have been. Be prepared to leave the field immediately if there is any deterioration of your condition.''

It was a joyful day for me and for our Moni friends when Gracie arrived back in Irian Jaya. By that time there were two nurses stationed with us at Hitadipa, Lorrie Farnsworth and Lois Belsey. They were assigned the job of routinely checking Gracie's blood pressure and keeping tabs on her health in general and reporting to the mission doctors.

There was neither deterioration nor improvement of the condition. Our goal of completing the translations still appeared to be attainable.

July 1984 came and with it the last Alliance field conference we would ever attend. Our colleagues honored us by having me speak at a men's breakfast and Gracie at a women's luncheon. On the final Friday night they had a farewell banquet for us with our son John (Zani Mala) as master of ceremonies. It certainly was a lovely occasion. Five years earlier, with the confidence of Caleb requesting the mountain of Hebron for an inheritance in the new land, we had assured our colleagues that we believed our God would enable us to hang on to finish the job. He had done exactly that.

Conference over, we returned to Hitadipa. We estimated that by April 1985 the translation would be completed and that before our departure we would have the opportunity to visit some of the other stations of our field.

Then one morning in October, as we listened at the Alliance broadcasting time on the two-way radio, a young woman at the office in Jayapura came on: "Hitadipa-Jayapura. Stand by for traffic with 'Pura at the end of the roll call."

Her message was very puzzling. The field chairman, Harold Catto, would be landing at our station in about an hour. All of us wondered what could have come up that would necessitate a visit from the chairman. When the plane landed, I said, "Harold, we have all been wondering what sort of bombshell you've brought in your bag."

"Let's go up to your house and I'll tell you about it," he said.

Bombshell it was indeed! The message was that acute homesickness had erupted in the heart of our daughter Faith. She later told us that she had been sending us warning signals for a long time, but said we had ignored them.

Gracie flew out to the office in Jayapura so she could talk to the school by phone. Their message was, "Faith needs you. Come as soon as you can."

Gracie could not take a national translation helper with her to Malaysia. She could do some work on her own, but all of it would have to be gone over carefully with a national when she returned home, and who knew when that would be? She hoped to be able to leave Faith after a few weeks, but one does not undo several years of emotional stress in a single fortnight. It became obvious that Faith couldn't handle any more

1ool. There was nothing for Gracie to
that when she and Faith arrived back
here would still be time for her to get
tne work done. The authorities kindly let Faith
leave several weeks early and still get full credit
for her semester's work. She and Gracie were
back in Hitadipa a few weeks before Christmas.

It seemed that the enemy was furiously trying to
throw every possible obstacle in our path. Faith
came down with hepatitis and all its debilitating
symptoms. The itching almost drove her mad.
Week after week she lay listlessly on the couch
needing much attention from us to keep her
spirits up. We took turns reading to her and tried
to think of surprises that would bring a little joy
into her life. The hepatitis dragged on and on and
with it the translation program.

There certainly wouldn't be any time to visit
other stations before we left. Prospects looked
more and more grim for finishing the translation.
Perhaps we could postpone our departure by six
weeks?

But there was one snag. Because of visa regula-
tions, Faith had to leave the country by June 4, so
even though the rest of us had permanent visas,
June 4 became our deadline as well.

29

Task Completed!

NOT ONLY WAS IT NECESSARY for the New Testament to be completely revised but the translation work on the Shorter Old Testament had to be finished. The United Bible Societies required the submission of three perfect copies of the manuscript.

I am not a good typist, but I cut all the stencils for the New Testament on our wide-carriage Olympia typewriter. It was a rare stencil that didn't have the blue carbon dotted with red correction fluid. I thought of the almost impossible job it would be to type three perfect copies: "I will make an error. I will pull back the first carbon, the first copy and the second carbon. I will erase the error on the second copy. Then I will push the second carbon in place, push the first copy forward and erase that. Finally I will erase the original and retype the word. If I make an average of five errors per page as I did cutting the stencils, it will take about 20 years to produce the sort of manuscript that is required." What a prospect that was!

We had returned to the field for our last term with an IBM Selectric typewriter for Gracie to use.

She typed manuscripts from which plates were made for offset printing by the Regions Beyond Missionary Union's press. It would be frightfully expensive to pay air freight on fuel to run our diesel-electric generator all day in order for her to type. So we installed an inverter which produced a 110-volt alternating current from 12-volt batteries that were recharged as our diesel ran during the evening hours. Operating an electric typewriter with a makeshift power supply is not too precarious because an interruption of power doesn't erase several hours of tedious work. As other missionaries testified, using computers under such circumstances could be a very frustrating experience.

Ann Grinnell, one of the Alliance missionaries working in our Jayapura office, had received special training in computers during her last furlough and was given the task of computerizing the accounting department. In addition, the office hired an Indonesian woman, Betty Pattipeluhu, also experienced in computers, to be Ann's assistant.

I had heard how computers could drastically reduce the time required for translation projects and, during a trip to Jayapura, met with Ann. "Ann, I see no way that I can finish revising the New Testament and prepare a manuscript acceptable to the Bible Society during the time remaining in this term. I realize that your schedule is very full, but would your new Indonesian assistant possibly have time to put the New Testament on the computer?"

"Bill, I want to give any help I can toward getting your job done," she replied. "I will talk to Betty and see if she is willing to keyboard a language that is completely unfamiliar to her."

Not long after my return to the station, a note came from Ann. "Betty is willing to key in your translation, Bill. Send out a section for her to work on."

Following is an excerpt from the letter I wrote in reply:

> Dear Ann,
>
> It is a real thrill to be sending you the first few pages of Matthew to be put on the computer. As I do it, I want to thank you ever so much for your encouragement during conference and later on at Jayapura. It is a life-long dream beginning to come true—the New Testament under one cover.

Ann's reply was encouraging:

> Betty really enjoys the translation work more than anything else we ask her to do. And she is so alert while keyboarding it that often if there is a misspelled word, even though she doesn't understand Moni, she picks it up. She is always very faithful and loyal about her work and it gives her a special sense of joy to know that she is working on the Scripture.

Betty bravely accepted everything I sent her. There were pages of new revisions, typed, but full of corrections. There were recently mimeographed booklets to be inserted at the specified places. There were older booklets with extensive revisions of the original text. Betty keyboarded whatever copy I sent her, ran it off on the printer and mailed the printouts back to us. In the beginning there were quite a few errors, but we were amazed at the way the errors decreased with each new portion she returned.

But what about the Shorter Old Testament, parts of which Gracie was still translating? Friends at home had sent money to the field so that the RBMU Press at Sentani could print it. But what they were turning out was one booklet at a time. Would the Moni preachers have to make do with a separate booklet for each book? Thus, the next question for Ann was, "Could Betty possibly take on this other enormous project as well?"

"Send them out and we'll do what we can," Ann replied.

By that time the office had another Indonesian worker, Silas Liborang, who had been trained as a computer operator. He was drafted to help Betty and soon every plane brought in reams of printouts for us to correct and return. When Silas was asked about his part in keyboarding the Moni Scriptures, his reply was: "Oh, I do only a very little. It is *Ibu* Betty's project." *Ibu*, literally *mother*, is a term of respect for a married woman.

The tempo of the race continued to accelerate

as the day of our departure drew closer. It was now only a matter of weeks, and there was no way that Gracie and I could finish all the things that had to be done before we could leave the field.

Again, the Lord sent us help from another quarter. Lorna Line, one of our fellow students at Nyack College many years before, offered to spend a couple of weeks with us. And what a blessing that was, for we had not fully realized the enormity of the task of sorting our belongings and getting them ready either to take with us or to leave in Irian Jaya. The sorting done, there was the job of making up packages that did not exceed the limits for weight and dimensions. Each package had to have cloth sewn around it to ensure its safety in transit. Then there was the preparation and placement of address labels. Lorna worked day after day from early morning until late at night while Gracie and I continued to check printouts and attempted to prepare the station for the time when lights would cease to shine from the windows of the Cutts's mission residence.

Bill Jr.'s graduation from the eighth grade in Sentani was to be on May 24th, just a few days before our deadline for leaving Indonesia. It was our plan to leave Hitadipa four days before the graduation exercises in order to correct the printouts of the manuscripts that had not yet come to Hitadipa.

Lorna was scheduled to leave six days before us. Two nights before her departure, Gracie said, "Bill, I have a strong impression that I should go out to Sentani with Lorna in order to work on those final printouts. With all the proofreading and correcting that needs to be done, I feel that going out on the day we planned will be cutting things too close."

"Well, Gracie, it's too late to request a flight for you, but if there is room, we will take that to be a clear indication of what our Lord wants you to do."

There was room! Up early each morning and working late into the night, Gracie searched for errors while Betty and Silas made the corrections and set the printers going, rolling out the final perfect copies.

Although Ann was a key instrument used by our Lord in that mad, headlong race against time, her summary of the part she played in the project is pure understatement: "Actually I can't really say I did anything to supervise the work. Essentially what I always did for either Betty or Silas was 'put out fires.' If they had problems with machines, or questions regarding format or procedure, they'd check with me. Maybe it's best to say that I was sort of a link between you folks and them. The 10 days Gracie was in the office were some of the most precious days of my missionary career. The realization that the project was nearing completion and of what it meant to you folks and to the Monis made a huge impression on me."

As day after day of feverish activity passed, nagging questions remained. Would the job be finished before Bill's graduation exercises on Saturday evening? What about Monday? If the job was finished by the end of Monday, could we still take care of all the last-minute details and finish our packing on Tuesday? Could we be ready for Wednesday's departure time?

Saturday afternoon. The last error on the last printout was corrected on the last of the 24 disks. The "print" key was depressed. A shout of praise went up to the Lord. The task was completed! A couple of hours before the graduation exercises, a mission car rolled into Sentani with Gracie and all the corrected printouts.

Graduation exercises over, we boarded the Garuda Airlines plane to Jakarta. Among other precious things in our suitcases were packages containing 66 pounds of computer printouts for the New Testament and the Shorter Old Testament in the Moni language. In a few days they would be sent from Jakarta to the Indonesian Bible Society headquarters in Bandung.

On this earth we would never again see the people with whom we had spent 35 years of our lives. But by the power of the sovereign God working through the "weak thing" and his faithful companion, Gracie, we were leaving them a priceless gift—God's love letter to the Monis in their own language.

E p i l o g u e

Bill and Gracie still remember how painful it was to separate themselves from the tribe they had loved and served for over 35 years. At the farewell given by the tribe in their honor, an elderly man noted in his farewell address: "Most missionaries who retire leave their people alone with no help, but Tuani and Mama Cutts are leaving us a part of themselves. They have left us their son, John."

John Cutts, Zani Mala, was the first second-generation missionary with The Christian and Missionary Alliance in Irian Jaya.

• If you were inspired by reading *"Weak Thing" in Moni Land*, why not give copies to your friends? Additional copies are available from Christian Publications by calling toll-free **1-800-233-4443**. Let *"Weak Thing" in Moni Land* touch other lives as well.

• *"Weak Thing" in Moni Land* is the second book in a continuing collection of missionary biographies. For more information on ordering other titles in the *Jaffray Collection of Missionary Portraits*, call Christian Publications toll-free **1-800-233-4443**.

• If you would like your name added to our *Jaffray Collection of Missionary Portraits* mailing list, fill out and clip the form that follows and mail it to:

Christian Publications
3825 Hartzdale Drive
Camp Hill, PA 17011

Christian Publications will notify you when a new *Jaffray Collection* title is available.

☐ Yes! Please add my name to your *Jaffray Collection of Missionary Portraits* mailing list.

Name _____

Address _____

City _____ State ____ Zip _____

WC2